The Debt Trap

America's Path From Superpower To Debtor State

GEW Intelligence Unit

Global East-West, London

Contents

1

Introduction

Understanding The Debt Trap

Explaining Debt Trap: An Economic Analysis

Sovereign debt is the quintessential characteristic of contemporary economics influencing the international financial system. The idea of a debt trap based on economic reasoning refers to a situation when a country cannot administer or pay off its debt and resorts to continually borrowing to pay interest on obligations and payments. Policymakers, economists, and citizens must grasp this issue's depth. Historically, the debt trap has afflicted several civilisations, with some accounts going back to ancient times. The ability to borrow money to finance public or military expenditures led to debilitating debt that contributed to their downfall. While the contours have changed in modern times, the debt trap still manifests itself in several ways, moulding the economic and fiscal policies of many countries worldwide. The whole system of government spending, tax policies, monetary policies, international trade and investment, and several other external factors come into

play and contribute to this phenomenon. Moreover, the consequences, such as currency depreciation, rise in interest rates, inflation, and overall economic stability, are equally or perhaps more
alarming. One risk is facing a financial crisis without anticipating
and preventing the potential of a debt trap.

Understanding the intricate interplay of macroeconomic indicators, debt-to-GDP ratios, and their history highlights the dangers of national borrowing. Additionally, identifying unsustainable debt levels is crucial for formulating sound fiscal policies and
strategies for debt management. As further analysis is done, it is
clear that the effects of a debt trap go beyond a country's economic
health. Its social and political life, as well as its international standing, also suffer. Thus, the strategy to avoid a debt trap should be
accompanied by detailed planning to defend against a potential
financial disaster.

The Evolution of Sovereign Debt: A Brief History

Like other types of debt, sovereign or government debt has a
history that dates back numerous centuries, considering the rise
and fall of entire empires, their market systems, and even their
meticulously constructed financial markets. To grasp the modern
staggering multilayered web of international debt, it is vital to go
back in time and painstakingly analyse the history of sovereign
borrowing. Most modern debt can be traced back to older societies
like Mesopotamia, where ancient rulers would fund their military
campaigns and public works projects by taking loans from temples.
This primitive form of debt was the foundation for state borrowing and repayment obligations. Modern sovereign debt is said to
originate from European monarchs and their need for funds. One

of the most prominent examples is when the Venetian government began issuing bonds in the 13th century to fund its military. Suffice it to say that as mercantile trade grew, sovereign borrowing gave rise to organised markets and formal debt instruments. The increase in borrowing by sovereign nations that emerged during the Napoleonic Wars and World War I was uniquely unprecedented, signifying the birth of government debt as an essential facet of contemporary economic administration. Nations needed international cooperation to relieve their systematically restructured debt burdens after these conflicts rich in spending. Further redefining the scope of sovereign debt was the Great Depression, along with World War II, when governments adopted deficit spending policies to stimulate recovery and support wartime efforts. In the post-World War II era, the reconstruction of economies that had been ravaged by war was accompanied by unprecedented levels of multilateral lending and financial aid, which shifted the balance of sovereign lending power towards institutions like the IMF and International World Bank because of the newly defined dependency on these institutions for sustainable lending to aid economic growth. Nowadays, sovereign debt is subject to the challenges and opportunities posed by the internationalisation of finance, sophisticated financial instruments, and globalisation of capital, which has altered the approach to managing national debt.

The historical account of sovereign debt is not just a record of financial transactions, but a narrative that intertwines with world events and economic shifts alongside the history of mankind. It offers unique perspectives on the challenges of debt and the management of societal payments within contemporary civilisation. Understanding this historical context is crucial for gaining a comprehensive view of sovereign debt and its implications.

Quantifying Debt: Metrics and Modifiers

Sovereign debt is a complex concept that exists in multiple dimensions, making it challenging to define and systematically arrange. In the context of a country's policy, estimating its debt requires a comprehensive approach that considers several metrics and modifiers. This section outlines the process of quantifying such debt by identifying its basic components and the metrics that influence it. A holistic understanding of these factors is crucial for determining the well-being of a nation's finances.

Debt measurement approaches must incorporate different methods to appreciate its magnitude and consequences. For example, a country's economy is measured in its Gross Domestic Product (GDP), which also serves as a standard for its debt offering. A nation's lending is quantitatively expressed in a debt-to-GDP ratio, which becomes a qualitative parameter indicating the ability to meet the obligations borne out of the debt. In addition, the debt burden of a country and its citizens may also be looked at by individual citizens, known as per capita debt.

Evaluating the impact of debt requires consideration of its structure, including what types of debt compose the total. Dividing external and domestic debt reveals potential risk factors and sources of vulnerability tied to the debt. In addition, classifying debt into short-term and long-term provides vital information about repayment periods and their risks.

When estimating debt, it is most helpful to discuss the modifiers that could change the implications of the debt being considered. Changes in interest rates are critical for determining the level of debt and the cost necessary to service it. The value of debt is also susceptible to the forces of inflation and deflation, which change the burden placed on the economy. For countries with large amounts of foreign currency debt, changes in exchange rates yield great impacts.

When estimating debt, it is crucial to consider the broader context of the problem, which is significantly influenced by the political and socio-economic environment. The balance of payments and the discipline exercised on government spending are critical factors that need to be analysed to estimate the servicing costs of sovereign debt. Understanding a country's productivity and demographic structure is also essential for grasping the economic environment at the time of estimation. This emphasis on the broader context of debt estimation helps the audience appreciate the multifaceted nature of sovereign debt and its deep effects on various economies and the international financial system.

As in any effort that requires quantifying debt, it is essential to consider a variety of measurements and indices for a complete quantification. This part seeks to prepare readers through qualitative and quantitative dimensions so that they can evaluate sovereign debt and appreciate its strong effects on various economies and the international financial system from multi-faceted perspectives.

Structural Causes: Policy Decisions and Economic Changes

The sovereign debt crisis stems primarily from the interaction of a nation's policies and economic shifts. Regarding developing effective remedies and reducing potential risks, debt control requires an understanding of its structural causes. Policy decisions based on political thinking often determine the boundaries within which a country's economy is nurtured. Government decisions regarding welfare, military spending, and taxation can lead to considerable increases in debt. Also, shifts in the economy, such as recessions, inflation, and technological disruptions, often add to the burden of debt a nation carries. These shifts challenge policymakers who must balance sustaining economic growth and managing a country's fiscal policies. For instance, the deregulation of financial markets has historically been associated with higher levels of debt, speculative bubbles, systemic financial crises, and substantial expenditure of public resources. Population changes, particularly the aged and associated spending on entitlement, also constitute long-term problems that must be addressed. Trade and globalisation could also impact domestic industries and employment, which will affect social safety net spending and revenues.

Understanding the mechanisms behind the accumulation of debt helps us make sense of the intertwining relationship between shifts in policy decisions and economic activity. Understanding these structural elements allows us to design sophisticated approaches that respond to the core problems instead of tackling the surface-level problems. In the following sections, we will look into specific case studies and quantitative evidence illustrating how particular policies, in conjunction with other economic activities, have influenced the debt profile of a nation. The primary objective of this analysis is to dissect the fundamental components of sovereign debt and their relations and construct sound policies that rapidly respond to the permanent reality of the debt trap.

Debt Dynamics and Economic Cycles

When considering national debt, exploring the relationship between debt dynamics and economic cycles is essential. Tension between these factors exists, yet one finds it valuable, especially from a policymaking or civic standpoint, to disentangle them. As with many relations, it begins with an underlying principle: the nature of economic activity and public debt. When observing an economy, there is usually a boom phase followed by periods of contraction. As previously noted, tax revenues almost always increase during expansionary periods while the demand for social safety nets declines. This situation tends to create surpluses, increasing cash reserves or 'fiscal space', enabling debt reduction or prepayment. On the contrary, tax receipts tend to fall in the downturn or recession phases, leading to increased unemployment and necessitating higher government spending on welfare and various social stimulus programmes. All these conditions exacerbate the situation. Therefore, every deficit spent tends to accumulate credit while simultaneously driving growth into further deficit. The issuance of currency, weakened by such meagre conditions, loses value.

Overall, the economic activity cycle directly relates to a country's fiscal health. But that's not where the story ends. The national debt, too, can serve as a cyclical buffer, affecting the intensity and length of economic swings during both expansionary and contractionary phases. An increase in these constraints tends to limit a government's operational latitude during downturns while hindering counter-cyclical spending designed to boost recovery.

High debt servicing costs can further stifle productive public investments, dampening the prospects for long-term economic growth. Conversely, a lower debt burden and enhanced debt management enable increased fiscal space, allowing for a more prudent response to economic shocks. However, a more fundamental issue requires attention: the intricate relationship between debt and debt cycles. Strategic planning requires understanding the consequences of accumulating debt during periods of growth and the burden of sustaining that debt during periods of contraction. This plane is essential for a balanced economy that guarantees a sustained economic equilibrium in growth and stability. To tackle these challenges successfully, it is critical to move away from oversimplified claims and work to understand the complex net of relationships between national debt and economic cycles.

The Psychological Impact of National Borrowing

The effect of national debt is more than just its financial impact; in today's world, it also has psychological ramifications. National borrowing plays a pivotal role in shaping public opinion, and sentiment affects almost all aspects of life. Government debt, for instance, tends to generate worry, fear, distress, and other negative feelings towards the economy. As part of this phenomenon, people become more anxious and frightened about the government's future and Society's welfare, primarily because they do not believe there is a limit to the country's debt. The common person directly dealing with such debt may suffer from anxiety and stress because of the burden this will place on their future earnings. Servicing such debt carries a burden of responsibility that the average citizen feels is owed to society and shifts the conversation towards fairness and social debt. Additionally, the mere argument associated with

the accruing of debt on its own through political and media channels makes people view the gap between managed and misman-
aged funds and policies more profoundly, further showing in the
government's perception amongst the citizens.

As the stress of national debt capacity increases, it impacts public perception, further eroding public trust towards policies, institutions, and governance systems and weakening the social contract
with leadership. Given these psychological factors, governments
need to go beyond managing the economic aspects of their fiscal
responsibilities and work actively to address the negative mental
effects of owing money. Recognising the emotional consequences
of national borrowing provides decision-makers with an important tool to justify debt management plans, encourage public engagement in supporting fiscal policy, and actively restore confidence in the economy's perceived scalability. In addressing the
emotional aspects of sovereign debt, governments attempt to foster a sense of responsibility and solidarity while reducing citizens'
mental burdens due to national debt.

Public Perception: How Society Views Government Debt

Understanding Public Perception: The Key to Effective Fiscal Policy Public perception of debt is a powerful force in shaping
fiscal policy and maintaining economic stability. This perception,
influenced by a nation's history, political discourse, media, and
personal finances, is a crucial factor for economists seeking to navigate the complexities of sovereign debt management. It creates a
diverse array of perspectives, each with its own unique implica-

tions for policy.

Mildly public-charged sentiment focuses on accessibility, highlighting that there is no greater financial driving force than the government, creating boundless measures to assist the future economy in a sheltered suffocating network and spend drives assistance knee-wedging shift-and-loan mark zero for the intergenerational keel. "Spin" motivated investments cum moral debt mix begs for sentiments to arouse growth welfare in opposition. On the other hand, critical expansion policies oppose bareboat deontological spending die-hards always ready to indiscriminately austeritize expenditure in an insufficient response to overhung needs.

The people amazed by the surrogates of the economy are captivated by the spin while heading off, only to sit glued until the cheque comes. A captive audience straddled by conflicting dictates sweeping together gaped-eyed broth multi-bolded dictate steal cringing policies boldfaced shift-away-use scenario.

Furthermore, the circulation of basic economic concepts, such as fiscal responsibility, budget deficits, or debt-to-GDP ratios, affects the level of engagement and understanding the public develops toward these crucial matters.

Public perceptions of government borrowing are significantly influenced by individuals' experiences with personal financial management. Concerns about a nation's fiscal condition tend to peak during economic downturns, unemployment, and inflation, leading people to scrutinise government spending and debt. Conversely, robust economic growth tends to assuage public anxiety about public debt and bolster confidence in the country's economic prospects, fostering a sense of hope and optimism.

Moreover, societal perceptions of government borrowing are closely associated with dominant cultural values and beliefs about the extent to which the government should be involved in the economic welfare of its citizens. Different historical and geopolitical contexts have fostered varying attitudes towards accumulating debt. Some societies adopt active government policies during times of crisis, whilst others advocate for a more austere approach with limited state intervention.

As this work demonstrates, public perceptions of government debt are a complex interplay of socio-demographic and economic factors, sparking constructive debates and discussions. Addressing these perceptions requires nuanced policy designs and effective strategies tailored to different societal groups. This approach fosters a sense of engagement and empowerment, promoting informed decision-making and collective understanding of the intricacies of national debt.

Fiscal Responsibility vs. Economic Growth

The balance between fiscal responsibility and economic growth remains elusive for policymakers and economists. This issue encompasses how the government's finances should be managed without halting the potential for a vigorous economy. On the one hand, fiscal responsibility includes looking after public funds, managing budget deficits, and balancing the books to achieve stability in the future. Making choices about taxation, government spending, and debt accumulation to achieve reasonable or healthy public finances is very painful. The pursuit of fiscal discipline is often considered something that, in turn, creates barriers to opportunities for economic growth. Economically sustainable expansion is important to enhance the number of jobs available, the wealth level, and the finances required for public services. Achieving that desirable balance between both sides is no easy task, which often demands consideration of trade-offs, synergies, and careful deliberation. The interplay between fiscal responsibility and economic growth is also multicausal and multicentric, tracking the multitude of indicators and growth drivers shifts rapidly. Too much austerity can help balance the budget, but from then on, they will automatically grow the deep roots of social hardship and inequality.

On the other hand, ignoring fiscal policy is likely to foster short-term economic growth. Conversely, optimally managing economic activities over time can lead to sustained long-term economic yield; hence, infrastructure, education, and other vital sectors must be attended to even if they cause an imbalance in short-term deficits. Furthermore, sound governance entails crafting fiscal policy responsive to macroeconomic activity so that the policies do not overly restrict growth when the economy is depressed and do not allow the economy to run too hot during expansionary phases. Managing and mitigating fiscal discipline together with maintaining robust economic growth combines dual objectives that are layered, multifaceted, and interrelated, as it requires having a deep understanding of the current situation and anticipating the future. Looking back allows us to understand complex interactions between economic activities across different countries and enables us to understand policies that construct sustainable growth coupled with reasoned fiscal control.

Multimedia Case Studies: Debt Management

Identifying the balance between responsibility and growth is multifaceted. We all face the same problem: complexities associated with managing or relieving debt. This section explores case studies on how diverse nations approach debt strategies, who did what, their outcomes, and what lessons can be learned. The most popular studies will include Japan's attempt to recover from an enormous public debt during a recession, Germany's debt management within eurozone competition, and Canada's handling of budgetary pressures and growth simultaneously. Every case study is conducted with a keen focus on policy reactions, structural changes, international consequences and enduring economic viability. By studying these examples of debt management, readers will encounter varying approaches countries have taken, realising the aggressiveness of the nature of national debt. In addition, analysing the examined case studies will enable the identification of common blunders and the most effective ways to understand the intricacies of national debt. By reviewing many real-world situations, this section provides readers with the appropriate concepts and analytical frameworks to grasp the link between debt management and economic growth effectively.

Preparing for Deeper Explorations

While considering the additional aspects of the nation's debt and expenditure control, some preliminary analytical graphics done previously need to be explained. The following chapters will discuss the multi-layered aspects and consequences of the increasing national debt and foster a holistic approach to understanding this complex challenge in its complete context. We intend to offer the appropriate insights, which blend with research outcomes, historiography, and analysis.

This excerpt introduces the traditional economic and political theories and the social consequences of the increasing debt burden on the nation. It prepares for the overarching evaluation of the particular policies and their effects on the sustainability of public finances and economic growth. Analysing these issues on the anchor of such a constructed theory helps explain the intricacies of debt movements and their relation to reactions in the system and environment, in addition to macroeconomics.

In addition, in our later explorations, we will journey through different case studies from various parts of the world, focusing on successful debt alleviation endeavours, inspiring and cautionary tales, and critical debt-legacy turning points that affect modern-day debt policies. This approach will teach and aid in understanding the lessons needed for economists, policymakers, and even educated citizens.

Engaging in these further explorations requires attention to detail and critical thinking aimed at synthesising a wide array of information, analysing proposed policies, and considering the opportunity costs accompanying debt financing. This calls for an interdisciplinary approach and an attempt to disentangle public finance and monetary and political economics since the nature of debt is multifaceted and does not confine itself within the borders of academic silos.

Of course, the rest of our analyses encourage deep thought for the readers and other users interacting with the book content as it engages them with the complex nature of accumulating debt, sustainability considerations, and the implicit need for fiscal responsibility. The ultimate goal for the authors is to rekindle productive discourse surrounding the complex problem of achieving and maintaining long-term fiscal sustainability in a deeply intertwined world.

This part prepares us for an insightful exploration of national debt's intricate and complex geography, setting the mental framework for active and deeper interaction with the important challenges and possibilities present in our changing financial reality.

2
The Rise of US Debt
Historical Perspectives

Colonial Roots: The Birth of American Debt

The spending patterns in colonial America were integral in determining how the United States would manage future debts. In the earlier days of the colonies, the economy was agrarian, which resulted in no unified monetary system and thus hindered the economy's growth compared to other nations. Often, colonial governments resorted to accruing debt by borrowing money to finance public works and infrastructure projects, essentially creating a pattern of debt that was set to persist throughout American history.

The expansion and usage of credit in promissory notes and various types of colonial scrip forged a new pathway for issuing what was to become known as government-backed circulating bonds.

Public banks also started to surface at this point, providing an infrastructure for formalised lending and currency issuance. Regardless, colonial economies had severe problems related to inflation and counterfeiting regarding these new financial instruments.

The over-reliance on European borrowing significantly intertwined colonial prosperity with external debt, weakening the colonial stance during economic downturns and bringing about geopolitical conflict. These conflicts, alongside the economic turmoil, subjected American society to an unprecedented experience. The strain of repaying peacetime and wartime peculiar loans subjected American society to multi-generational spins of conflicting debts, leading to vitality-instilled debts.

Debt during the colonial period in America serves as a warning regarding the interdependence of a country's fiscal policy, economic growth, and sovereignty. The stresses of colonial finances outline the need to put context with modern debt analysis in examining the histories and forces that sculpt contemporary socio-political landscapes.

The Revolutionary War and Early Financial Struggles

The Revolutionary War heavily impacted the history of America, and as a new nation, America had to bear the costs of financing the war. The colonies had to take loans to support the military. To pay the military and other expenses, the Continental Congress had to issue bills of credit, which included 'continentals'. This could have been avoided without adequate taxes, but rampant currency overprinting led to hyperinflation. The war also worsened the fragile economy as the inflationary environment caused further disruption to trade and agricultural activities.

Post-war, America was struggling with loans from the Federal government and individual states. This economic burden only exacerbated the problem, especially considering that the Federal government did not have adequate taxation laws. The states were already in huge debt from the war. The economy was struggling without any structured debt policy, which meant there had to be some framework through which money could be efficiently funnelled into the economy and used to avoid the economic depression looming overhead like a dark cloud. Then, people realised that America was heading towards absolute collapse without a sufficient, structured medium to manage public debt.

These problems led to the drafting of the Constitution, a pivotal moment in American history. The Constitution allowed the Federal government to impose taxes, a crucial tool in managing the war debt and ensuring the country's financial stability.

Creating a centralised fiscal authority has allowed the country to deal with its national debt while minimising the chances of another financial crisis. Furthermore, under Alexander Hamilton in 1791, the First Bank of the United States was established to manage the national debt and stabilise the economy. This strategic move reassured the nation and its citizens, demonstrating a strong central government that could manage public finances, the precursor to modern fiscal policy and a guide to the country's economic growth.

As noted, the Revolutionary War and its consequences played a major role in determining the fiscal direction of the United States. The nation's early encounters with financial difficulty set the stage for a shift in the governance of the economy and institution-building aimed at guaranteeing fiscal stability. These initial years demonstrated the need for disciplined public money management and marked the beginning of a more developed and integrated financial system.

Civil War and Reconstruction: Financial Strain on a Divided Nation

The Civil War and Reconstruction period was one of the most difficult eras in American history, not due to the countless casualties it incurred but the burden of finances. Economically, it was an expensive affair for the Northern and Southern states, as each simultaneously endured significant costs in sustaining their militaries and economies. Economically, the South suffered more severely as they experienced a blockade which crippled trade for them and drastically increased inflation, worsening the situation further. It has also been noted that the defeat of Confederate states added a massive toll to the already fragile economy of Southern states by shattering poverty-stricken infrastructure. Lincoln's efforts to ease the financial burden of the Union by taking loans, introducing bonds, and national income tax in 1861 only added to their subscribed debt, which post-war would become dire fiscal pressure for them.

Even with the economic challenges the South faced throughout the war, the loss of trade crippled their economy during these times. The defeat of the Confederate states added to the burdening debt of the already fragile economy of Southern states, exacerbating the financial strain along with the need to rebuild poverty-stricken infrastructure.

The process of Confederate reconciliation into the Union made Reconstruction more difficult because it required significant federal resources for the South's recovery.

The Reconstruction era posed a daunting challenge in balancing the South's post-war spending with debt to rebuild the nation's economy. The Southern economy, devastated by the Civil War, forced the federal government to deal with outstanding debts while concurrently funding economic stimulus projects, such as infrastructure development and agricultural subsidies. The creation of the Freedmen's Bureau highlighted Reconstruction's varied dimensions by showcasing the government's efforts to aid freed slaves. Moreover, the intense political debates about issuing greenbacks to promote economic growth after the War added to the tension surrounding financial policy during the recovery period.

Straining US finances during the Civil War and Reconstruction profoundly transformed perceptions of fiscal policy and public debt, leaving deep scars on the US economy. Today's discussions about public policy, specifically state intervention and the economic power of national debt, have been influenced by the lessons of this period's fiscal turmoil.

The Great Depression: Economic Turmoil and Rising Indebtedness

The most challenging period in American history occurred during the 1930s. Alongside widespread unemployment, economic challenges, and the collapse of financial systems—all characteristics of the Great Depression—it stood out as one of the most trying times for Americans.

The devastating stock market crash 1929 took a heavy toll on the economy and served as a precursor for what was to come. With businesses closing down, an alarming number of banks failing, and farmers suffering from severe financial losses, the federal government's ability to deal with the crisis was tested. The enormous economic crisis greatly decreased tax revenues, worsening the national debt. As a result, the federal government faced severe constraints regarding funding critical relief efforts and public works projects. The New Deal policies of President Franklin D. Roosevelt and initiatives such as the Works Progress Administration and the Tennessee Valley Authority aimed to remedy the situation but at the cost of adding to the already crippling debt. Social welfare programmes like Social Security were also introduced during this period, which transformed the federal government's role in its citizens. There was a pressing need to intervene to reduce suffering and stimulate the economy, but that's where the concerns regarding the sustainability of incurring more debt arose.

The economic imbalance of the Great Depression, together with government policies and growing debt, remains relevant as a focal example for contemporary fiscal policy and public debt management laws.

World War II and the Post-War Boom: Debt Dynamics

The Second World War profoundly changed America's debt structure, setting the course for the country's economic growth on a completely new path. This adopted changes towards government spending, which caused a huge increase in the country's debt. By the war's end, America's national debt reached a historical peak, exceeding over 100% of GDP.

There was a remarkable shift in the economy's structure. After the world's superpowers started fuelling economic growth through modernisation, rising industrial production units using technology and robots, and surging consumer demand for new products, America experienced an extreme boom. All this enabled the government to earn more revenue; therefore, parents could lower the debt ratio to GDP.

The US Marshall Aid programme further highlighted the power behind the American economy after the Euro-war reconstruction and reinforced its position worldwide. However, spending on sustaining external commitments and defence continues to be high, creating new national debt burdens.

Created in 1944, the Bretton Woods Agreement was pivotal in constructing a monetary system for the world post-war. The US dollar was trade and finance's main international reference currency during this period. While the US capitalised on this system, it later struggled with controlling balance of payments surpluses, deficits, and exchange rates.

The adoption of conflicting policies characterised the post-war period. Domestically, they wanted to achieve growth but internationally stabilise relations with other countries and eliminate the debt burden left over from the war. In the coming decades, that mixture of social, political, and economic priorities resulted in a balancing act between spending and trying to implement a coherent economic stability strategy.

The transformational period of the US economy showcased how much leverage the country had in international debt. Having an enormous amount of debt at their disposal showcased strength in long-run growth. The intensity of US fiscal pressures, combined with shifts in global geopolitics, would change the trajectory of US debt.

Bretton Woods and the Dollar's Global Role

The Bretton Woods Conference in 1944 was a significant financial event, leading to the US dollar's international role within the monetary system. During this landmark conference, delegates from 44 Allied countries came to New Hampshire to create a post-World War II economic blueprint that would provide stability while avoiding the economic chaos of the inter-war period. The conference led to the creation of the International Monetary Fund (IMF) and the World Bank, whose aims were to bolster cooperation, aid adjustment of international monetary relations, and facilitate the reconstruction and development of the world after the War. However, the decision concerning pegging world currencies to the dollar and fixing its valuation to gold determined its long-standing impact. At that time, the US possessed most of the gold reserves, so it practically crowned the dollar as the backbone of the global financial system. Under the Bretton Woods system, the dollar was redeemable for gold at $35 per ounce for participating countries, hence maintaining fixed exchange rates with the dollar.

The "Golden Age of Capitalism" is characterised by an essential peak in economic activity straddled by a boom in international commerce and investment caused by the new financial order. At the same time, the US gained considerable power over global finance and commerce with the dollar's supremacy as the United States economy flourished, ushering in American dominance around the world. The Bretton Woods system, however, did not survive. In the late 1960s, the Vietnam War and rampant inflation began to strain the system's core terribly. It led to the crises culminating in Nixon's decision in 1971 to suspend the convertibility of

dollars to gold. This marked the end of the Bretton Woods framework, thus enabling the development of contemporary exchange
rate system floating mechanisms – considered today as today's
monetary regime. Today, nations at various stages of development
depend on the dominance of the dollar, while the US Bretton
Woods set in motion allows them to alter global commerce and
affect international finance.

The 1970s: Inflation, Energy Crisis, and Economic Stagnation

The 1970s proved to be a tumultuous decade for the USA's economy, as a multitude of issues plagued both micro and macro levels.
One of the most striking features of this era was the term "Stagflation," a unique combination of unemployment and inflation that
confounded economists and policymakers alike. Soaring energy
costs, unchecked government budgeting, and a mounting public
debt all contributed to the stagflation crisis, making it a particularly challenging period for the economy.

The 1973 oil crisis, triggered by OPEC's oil embargo on the
West in response to their support for Israel during the Yom Kippur
War, was a pivotal event that exacerbated inflation and slowed
growth. The sharp increase in oil prices had a devastating effect
on the global economy, leading to widespread unemployment and
rampant inflation. The United States, heavily reliant on imported
oil and vulnerable to supply shocks, was particularly hard hit by
the crisis.

The United States' oil crisis put another strain on the economy,
already suffering from large government spending and irrespon-

sible fiscal policies. The social and political matrix of the United States as of 1970 is represented by a drastic increase in the federal budget deficit due to military spending in the Vietnam War, various social programs aimed at the welfare state, and spiralling national debt. The economy was put under greater strain after the move to a fiat currency system in 1971, which led to rampant inflation and uncertainty regarding currency value. A fiat currency system is one where a country's currency is not backed by a physical commodity like gold, but rather by the government's declaration that it has value and can be used as a medium of exchange.

The government's attempts to relieve the economy only created greater issues due to the State of the existing labour market. Price inflation, coupled with increased wages due to unionisation, compounded the issue further, negatively impacting the purchasing power of the working middle class. Consumer inflation, coupled with soaring business costs, greatly decreased profits, leading to a hiring freeze and reduced economic development. All these events led to the deterioration of living standards and an overwhelming economic sense of stagnation in the middle class.

In light of these crises, policymakers tried to concoct a plan for restoring balance and stimulating growth. Some of the policies offered included managing policies like wage and price controls and more aggressive fiscal and monetary policies to stimulate employment and demand. The mixed results further illustrated the multifaceted problems that faced the country.

America's economic policies underwent a profound change in the decade after the 70s, which witnessed uncontrollable inflation and economic stagnation. The persistent inflation during this decade fundamentally shifted the US economy's guiding principles, providing insight into the adaptive capacity of institutions and leaders amidst formidable challenges. Today, there are ongoing

debates about the best ways to manage inflation, ensure energy security, or enable economic growth while balancing sustainability,
all of which can be traced back to the impacts of the 70s.

The End of the Gold Standard and Floating Currencies

In the course of the 20th century, the global economy faced numerous changes, which resulted in the abolishment of the gold
standard and the adoption of floating currencies. The Bretton
Woods system, which sought to stabilise international currencies
and promote trade growth in 1944, utilised fixed exchange rates
that were tied to the US dollar, which had a peg to gold. Problems
started to arise in the mid-1960s with the system when the US
could not sustain the selling of gold to dollars due to constant trade
deficit spending and depleting funds due to the Vietnam War.

The existing monetary system was rapidly being criticised for its
viability, and Nixon's administration made the call in August 1971
to suspend the dollar's convertibility to gold, effectively cutting
ties with the gold standard. This was monumental in the timeline
of global currencies and enhanced the free-floating system while
paving the way for fiat currencies.

The adoption of floating exchange rates created the most profound shift in international finance since the advent of the gold
standard. It instigated a dramatic increase in the degree to which
currencies could fluctuate relative to one another, facilitating
greater freedom in the implementation of monetary policies. In
addition to this newfound flexibility, governments gained the ability to strategically combat the adverse effects of economic reces-

sions and surrenders. Yet, the escalated friction between currencies led to turbulent market activity and distinctly heightened risks for multinational entities.

Moreover, the speculation of gold used in international transactions acted as a catalyst, enabling debates regarding an alternative pegged system to circulate more widely. Without fixed unitary set frameworks, central banks are free to problematise the goals and motives of maintaining a range of tolerance windows for steering monetary policy without suffering from excessive volatility detrimental to stability in currency markets.

Finally, international relations among different countries have further progressed due to the change in the consensus framework for international reserve currency. This phenomenon commenced an era in the history of international economics and politics that has been aggressively portrayed as being shaped by surpassing newly imposed restrictions on the modern era of international monetary relations.

Government Spending in the New Deal Era

The New Deal period featured significant government spending and active policies aimed at the mid-section of the American economy, especially during the presidency of Franklin D. Roosevelt in the 1930s. Roosevelt's administration attempted to overcome the dire economic challenges posed by the Great Depression by offering relief, recovery, and reform through extensive spending programmes, initiatives, and public works at the federal level. There was a marked change in the government's spending policy towards aggressive economic intervention. It led to the relief of a considerable number of unemployed Americans and the revamp of public infrastructure and institutions. As part of the New Deal, there was also the establishment of works and employment-providing schemes like the Works Progress Administration (WPA) and the Civilian Conservation Corps (CCC) meant to provide immediate relief. Besides these, social security measures were also introduced under the New Deal aimed at the most susceptible parts of the population to shield them from the brunt of economic hardships.

In addition, the period saw the introduction of certain protective measures, including establishing the Securities and Exchange Commission (SEC) and the Federal Deposit Insurance Corporation (FDIC), aimed at restoring public confidence in the financial system and averting future systemic collapses. The unprecedented growth in government expenditures during the New Deal period was instrumental in crafting the modern economic framework of the United States. Although the actions taken during this time were met with mixed responses and opposition, these policies fundamentally redefined the interplay between the government, the economy, and the citizenry. Even today, the debates on the optimal level of government intervention continue to permeate policy discourse. However, one dominant narrative remains the extravagant public spending associated with the New Deal and its effect on the understanding of fiscal policy in a historical context.

Pre-Reagan Fiscal Policies: Setting the Stage for Modern Challenges

The time before President Reagan came into power was an important shift in how the US implemented fiscal policies. Moreover, policies that would challenge the modern era were envisioned during this time. After World War II, the country started following Keynesian policies that focused on government intervention during certain phases of the economy, along with promoting capitalism. This was a positive shift for the US as it greatly increased investment in various sectors such as social programmes, infrastructure, healthcare, and welfare. Alongside this progress, the country began accumulating public debt due to military spending and international undertakings. The Vietnam War further strained these resources, causing the country to grow in deficits.

Additionally, during the 1970s, the economic situation worsened due to rising energy costs caused by wars in the Middle East. All these factors led to stagflation, a period of slowly increasing economic growth but high inflation. In response, policymakers tried to freeze wages and prices along with expansionary monetary policies, but these offered no tangible results. At the same time, the OPEC oil embargo put additional pressure on the economy, revealing its susceptibility to external shocks.

While these problems persisted, the federal government's fiscal imbalance only worsened, marking the beginning of the fiscal disaster that defined the Reagan period. The policy mix changed dramatically after Ronald Reagan's inauguration in 1981. Following supply-side economics, his administration aggressively cut taxes and deregulated industries to promote economic growth. Although meant to increase business and investment activity, these actions also marked a new period of persistent deficits and an ever-increasing national debt. During this time and in these particular shifts in fiscal policy, contemporary discussions over the need for taxation and entitlement policies and government intervention in the economy began. Additionally, it reframed the discussion of deficits and debt, shaping how future administrations would manage fiscal policy. The pre-Reagan era's policies are still felt today within economic policy frameworks, leading discussions on advancing sustainable economic growth, maintaining a reasonable level of fiscal responsibility regarding debt, and the balance needed between public spending and dynamism from the private sector.

3

Post-Reagan Era

Tax Cuts and Expanding Deficits

Reaganomics Revisited

Reaganomics, recently brought to the fore in public discussions, is associated with the supply-side economics of conservatism that emerged in the United States in the 1980s when President Ronald Reagan assumed office. He introduced the weakening of federal regulations on the business sector and tax cuts, significantly increasing the government's budget deficit and reducing its expenditures. The government subsidises private investments in economic growth, expecting the revenue growth resulting from spending to compensate for spending-side budget deficits. Excessive investment and entrepreneurship will lead to economic growth, bringing new revenues for the state. The economy will be revived concurrently with the rate of inflation. Inflation in the country, which was curbed moderately during the late 1970s, is also expected to decrease. This policy aims to create a new economic environment known as supply-side economics to lower the dollar price.

The above goals and policies of refraining from spending would fuel the economy, but the ever-mounting debt would remain unchecked. The surplus of unregulated taxation has made the rich richer while financially straining the lower class. The middle class would remarkably enable greater productivity and drive overall prosperity for everyone. Unabashed critiques of Reaganomics argue that the incessant socio-economic policies have resulted in exploding debt due to increased military expenditure. This system dramatically augments the staggering national debt. These sharp military spending have unchecked consequences on the country's increase in deficit. With Reagan now enabling rapid economic growth alongside boosting funds available to spend on social welfare programmes, the effects will allow for the free wielding of social spending to stimulate the economy, creating jobs and devastating consequences for the social infrastructure. Furthermore, the outcome has enabled people to shift the burden, continuing to cry, "for there's no place they can go harder than deficits." In essence, booming expenditures under the expansionary fiscal policies fuelled spending, further widening the gap in social inequality and fuelling the divide as they marched on, crowning the abuse of social and protective measures as social relief.

Analysing the consequences of Reaganomics is crucial for understanding the influence of 1980s economic thinking on contemporary policies. In this chapter, I will delve into the complex network of Reagan's economy, evaluating his policies and their impacts in the context of America's economic history. Reaganomics, with its unique blend of supply-side economics and tax cuts, has left a lasting imprint on theUS economy, shaping the trajectory of economic policies for years to come.

Tax Policy and Economic Theories of the 1980s

In the 1980s, tax policy, combined with economic theories, played a pivotal role in shaping the total expenditure of the United States. These years were marked by the rise of Reaganomics, a supply-side-driven approach championed by President Ronald Reagan. Supply-side economics posits that cutting taxes, especially for the wealthy and businesses, leads to increased savings, investment, and economic growth. The rationale behind these tax cuts was that they would boost productivity at the corporate level, leading to lower taxes and increased economic growth. The crux of this argument is that the ensuing economic growth, based on certain assumptions, would result in increased tax revenue to the government, thereby offsetting the losses from the tax cuts. As a result, the Reagan government made significant changes to the tax system, with the aim of fostering national economic growth and increasing employment.

The tax reforms mentioned above brought about several changes; for example, personal income tax rates and corporate taxes were lowered, and income tax brackets were adjusted to account for inflation. In addition, the 1981 Economic Recovery Tax Act significantly reduced marginal tax rates. After that, the Tax Reform Act of 1986 transformed the tax code into a simpler and more streamlined format, closing numerous loopholes. This resulted in a tax-neutral restructuring of revenue collection. These tax policies, as economically stimulating as they were, created frontrunners arguing that the policies only widened the gap between rich and poor, fiscally increasing the national debt.

And finally, during the 1980s, some contending economic ideologies emerged and transformed the focus of tax policy discourse. Adopting laissez-faire capitalism, known as libertarianism, gave rise to neoclassical economics, which features little to no government involvement in the economy, promoting deregulation and self-interest. At the same time, Keynesian economics, which centres around the work of John Maynard Keynes, emphasising the government's role in using fiscal and monetary policy to mitigate economic cycles and maintain low unemployment, emerged.

Combining these economic theories with tax policy raised debates on potential governmental intervention in the economy, questioning the appropriate degree of taxation and the actual effectiveness of supply-side economics. These discussions were felt throughout academic and political spaces and public conversations, greatly affecting tax policies and shaping future policies, too.

The 1980s served as a playground for testing radical theories on tax policies—the decade became a trial ground for bold tax policies. This decade's impact deeply influences modern tax reform discussions alongside economic stimulation, focusing on the balance between driving growth and responsible spending.

The Legacy of the 1986 Tax Reform Act

The Tax Reform Act of 1986 is one of the most comprehensiveUS tax code overhauls in history, enacted during the Reagan administration. It was designed to streamline the tax system, broaden the base, and reduce marginal tax rates for individuals and corporations. This landmark legislation enhanced economic growth, fairness, and international competitiveness. The 1986 tax reform eliminated many tax shelters, lowered tax rates, and expanded the tax base by closing loopholes. The Act sought to simplify the tax code and make it more equitable for all by reducing marginal tax rates while broadening the tax base. Notably, the Act reduced the top individual income tax from 50% to 28% and closed many corporate tax loopholes, setting a new standard for an efficient tax system. The 1986 Tax Reform Act impacted the economy and reshaped the national conversation on tax policy and fiscal responsibility.

The legislation prompted continued discussions concerning how taxation impacts economic behaviour and the design of the tax system. Moreover, this legislation created a new standard for cross-party cooperation in tax reforms—an approach later administrations tried to adopt. Despite the criticisms and complexities accompanying it, the 1986 Tax Reform Act marked a turning point in the history of tax policy in the United States. Its legacy is still in debates around tax reforms, economic policy, and the politics-policy nexus. Appreciating the implications of such landmark policies helps to understand how the United States tax system evolved and its relevance to the wider economy.

Deficit Expansion in the Late 20th Century

The latter part of the 20th century observed a dramatic increase in the federal deficit for the United States. A systemic mismatch between government spending and revenue collection during this period deepened the deficit. Some of the factors that contributed to this deficit expansion include rising spending on national defence, increasing costs associated with entitlement programmes, and tax policies that did not provide enough revenue for these spending increases. These trends during this period resulted in a heightened national debt, which was alarming given the long-term sustainability of the country's fiscal policies. Economically, politically, and socially, there was a lack of unity to focus on the factors driving deficit expansion in the late 20th century. There were significant increases in discretionary spending, especially in security and defence spending, that was further exacerbated by geopolitical changes in the Cold War and, later on, military conflicts. Further, the uncontrolled structural deficit attributable to mandatory entitlement spending due to ageing demographics and rising healthcare costs further worsened the fiscal imbalance. At the same time, there was a shift in the legislative environment that was more permissive to spending, making it more likely that calls for increased domestic spending would get more support than measures sought to reduce the deficit.

Furthermore, tax policies implemented during this period, such as cuts to income tax and other reforms, did not achieve sustainable revenue levels to close the growing budget gaps. Consequently, the gap grew too quickly, worsening anxiety about the country's financial future. This gap growth was felt across the economy, influencing other areas like interest rates, investment, and the general prospects of coming generations. In summary, the late 20th century marked a period of profound growth in the deficit of theUS federal budget, which resulted from an intricate mix of economic, political, and structural factors. Comprehending the reasoning for this defining moment in American history helps understand current fiscal debates and develop policies to proactively deal with future fiscal issues.

Political Dynamics: Influence of Legislative Changes

The political impact of legislative changes on fiscal policy and deficit spending in the 20th century was a thick web of inter-connected stories. Relations between the executive and Congress and the general political environment were very important for developing policy and fiscal planning and further widening the deficit. Bipartisan support and opposing parties' disagreements were equally important for the passage and enactment of legislation regarding tax and spending policies and for dealing with the deficit during this time.

The change in economic theories and their policy impacts was one of the underlying reasons for the changes in legislation. Supply-side economic policies, or Reaganomics, emphasised the need to lower taxes to stimulate investment and economic growth. This was also the rationale behind the Tax Reform Act of 1986, which sought to trim the tax base and marginal tax rates while attempting to simplify the tax code. As with all legislation, the Act adversely affected government revenue and the increasing deficit, illustrating the complex interdependence between legislative policy changes and fiscal policy results.

Furthermore, interest group politics must be examined critically in relation to lobbying and political influence while analysing the politics of legislation change. Industry groups, popular interest groups, and think tanks affiliated with political parties directly lobbied legislators to change spending and taxation policies to fit the tax and spending framework. The tail end of such influence often resulted in many appropriations that gave a favourable outcome for particular groups or constituents, which ultimately distorted the fiscal budgeting process.

Moreover, the internal power relations between Congress, particularly during periods of divided government, contributed to legislative output stagnation and intensive budget debates. The debates around reaching a compromise on comprehensive fiscal policies were deep-seated political disputes over discretionary spending, entitlement reforms, and politically sensitive budgetary lines.

In addition, previously undocumented external factors, such as international events and economic downturns, significantly strained policymakers' ability to manage growing deficits. This greatly complicated the underlying politics of any change in legislation, as modifications required swift and bold responses to the economy's unpredictable realities.

In the post-Reagan period, the complex relationship between politics, ideology, and economic forces dominated the scope and impact that changes in legislation could exert on fiscal discipline and public debt. The intricate relationships of these factors are essential to understanding the deepening deficits and the enduring consequences of the nation's post-recession policy choices in a broader context.

Economic Growth Vs. Fiscal Responsibility

The controversy concerning economic growth and vertical fiscal imbalance has drawn considerable attention in public policy and governance. Economic growth advocates suggest that "economic development on its own should be the key priority from which living standards are derived." They propose policies like tax rebates, deregulation, and infrastructure spending to promote economic activities and enhance employment opportunities. On the contrary, supporters focusing on fiscal responsibility highlight the need for a balanced budget and reduced government deficits. They express concerns regarding ultrahigh state spending, borrowing, and the increasing chances of interest rates and inflation. The dual problem becomes even more difficult when carefully studying the two sides of the coin, trying to discover a middle ground enabling policymakers to expand the economy while remaining within the limits of fiscal restraint.

In the past, times of economic growth were typically aligned with periods of increased government spending. This is because policymakers focus on increasing aggregate demand during a recession. At the same time, a failure to control deficit spending not matched by economic growth can offer a positive propensity for national debt, significantly endangering future generations. Additionally, growing debt levels tend to inflate borrowing costs, weaken the capacity to respond to future needs, and reduce private investments. On the other hand, stringent policies aimed at budgetary discipline may slow the economy, aggravating unemployment and income inequality.

The combination of sustainable economic growth and fiscal prudence is more complex due to external demographic changes, technological innovations, and shifts in international markets. Moreover, economists must consider entitlements, healthcare expenses, and pension responsibilities while crafting any forward-looking, sustainable fiscal policy. When considering the trade-offs, a balanced approach for short-term stimulus spending complemented with a long-term structural remedy to heal the foundation of fiscal resilience is recommended. The impact of a stimulus on expenditure limits must be balanced against an increase in the per capita debt burden on future generations.

The balance between economic augmentation and fiscal stew-
ardship requires analytic scrutiny, systematic policy approaches, and cross-party collaboration. To achieve a prudent balance
between the two, practical measures must be deployed to settle
short-term economic pressures against long-term solvency discipline. Keeping in mind the nuances of this concern, the following
section focuses on the government's expenditures on various welfare programmes and assesses their significance for the economy as
a whole.

Impact on Social Programs and Public Services

The urgent concern regarding social programmes and public
services arising from increasing deficits and national debt de-
serves thorough reflection. There is heightened public interest and
scrutiny given to allocating funds towards important social safety
nets and core public services as government funds are constrained
due to increasing fiscal pressures. This concern concerns the cap
placed on expenditures and the value derived from the populace
spread across varied social classes. The impact of budgetary limitations could be felt at multiple levels within the social structure
and affect citizens' lives in numerous ways.

The social programmes of healthcare, education, housing aid,
and welfare are sustainable only when sufficient funding is available. Increasing deficits and the need to curb spending often
risk the effectiveness and availability of these services. Shrinking
the budget allocated for social programmes can have dire consequences on the most impacted and underserved groups, making
inequality and suffering more intense. Cuts to the social spending

budget also include the maintenance of public goods like transport infrastructure and housing, which makes both development and safety more difficult to attain, especially for communities.

There is an added risk regarding the level of concern deemed healthy for society in the long term. More social unrest and worsened health skew demographic projections due to increased mortality are all attributable to insufficient public funding. Deep cuts to essential public services compromise the ability and motivation of a country's economy to function, resulting in an overly stressed fiscal burden. The public help combine to form a social contract which, when weakened alongside other forms of social assistance and protective services, leads people to become increasingly apathetic towards the functioning of the government.

Despite the issues, the circumstances provide opportunities for new policy innovations. Attempts to reorganise the delivery of social services, increase productivity, and reduce fiscal waste can lessen the damaging impact of austerity measures. Some critical public services may also be provided, in part, through public-private partnerships, community participation, or civic engagement initiatives. Establishing protective limits around social programmes and strategically managing the services' resources may help mitigate these demographic groups' risks while exercising financial responsibility.

Overall, the social programmes and services and public services offered as spending items in a budget should be managed for balance to enable smooth sailing even in worse fiscal conditions and turbulence. Thoughtful consideration accompanied by constructive debate and inclusive governance centred on citizens' priorities enables striking the balance of exercising fiscal control while actively maintaining and developing social infrastructures and services.

International Comparison: US Debt Strategies

Any country, including the United States, must consider the global benchmark when strategising the management of national debt. A global comparison reveals that the practices and policies adopted under debt management differ from one country to another owing to distinct political, economic, and historical factors.

Perhaps the most notable contrast relates to the acceptance level of public debt among developed countries. While some European regions have historically observed a more relaxed approach to public debt, the United States tends to be more accommodating towards debt accrual, especially during recessionary civilian demand or war. This particular difference is suspiciously quiet and raises fundamental concerns regarding public asset investment and enduring fiscal investment stability.

Another noteworthy issue to examine is the impact of the debt burden on the workings of international financial markets and the economy. Because the US dollar is the dominant reserve currency, the US is afforded a measure of latitude and control over the country's debt management. At the same time, however, this benefit poses additional dangers and problems because the increase and decrease in US debt levels tends to increase the volatility of international markets and affect the value of currencies. These relationships support the argument that one has to explain US debt policies in the context of the global economy.

Furthermore, in working with the efficiency of different debt alleviation policies, it is crucial to understand what other nations have done. Some of these economies, such as Canada and Australia, have recently pursued actively contractionary public debt policies to achieve a balanced budget and reduce government expenditures. In contrast, Japan has struggled with sustaining high debt relative to GDP, creating controversy on whether to use austerity or expansionary fiscal policy. The available approaches are useful regarding the likely outcomes and compromises one will make when adopting a debt management policy.

In the end, international analysis of US approaches to managing debt reveals a complicated interplay of economic philosophies, world politics, and history. By evaluating other countries' policies and their relative successes and failures, an informed debate on the best approach for sustainable policy can be developed, using insights from other nations to negotiate the complex reality of managing and fostering economic growth and debt.

Analysis of Long-Term Economic Indicators

In the US economy, an assessment of its debt, along with other economic indicators, needs to be put in context to see the economy's long-term trajectory. A policy framework approach seeks understanding the interrelationship among laws, policies, and the broader economy. One such case is looking at the historical data on GDP growth, inflation, and unemployment and using them to analyse the economy's current situation. This has to be looked at together with the debt-to-GDP ratio, which measures the nation's borrowing dependency. Analysing expenditures, revenue collection, and budget deficits offers important insights about government spending, increasing debt, and defaulting.

Along with population changes, shifts in entitlement programmes and the labour force enable a deeper understanding of long-term economic shifts. Together with productivity, technological change, and international trade, this enables an understanding of the position in which the US competes economically with other countries. Alongside shifts in investment and consumer spending, this helps create a better understanding of social changes and overall societal progress.

Equally important is an analysis of the financial markets' resilience alongside the banking institution's systemic level and the impact of regulations on the economy's ability to sustain itself. Finally, considering potential black swan phenomena, geopolitical threats, and eco-related issues from the above view on long-term economic development is essential to fully understand the economy. In contrast, such a multi-faceted view helps comprehend these economic indicators, highlights the underlying reality, and helps provide accurate advice to policymakers, business entrepreneurs, and the general public.

Conclusion: Lessons from the Post-Reagan Era

Reflecting on the post-Reagan period, it is abundantly evident how this period has impacted the economy of the United States. The lessons learned from this particular era seem to offer a deeper understanding of the nuances of fiscal policy and deficit management. One of the key lessons is balancing tax policies with deficit management. The period was marked by adopting supply-side economics with massive tax cuts to enhance growth and investment. The increasing budget deficits that followed highlighted the problems that arose when there was a lack of government spending control. This paradox warns policymakers and economists because it highlights the causal relationship between tax policies and deficit outcomes.

Additionally, the era demonstrated the chronic effects of policy enactment on the country's economic well-being. The consequences of something as impactful as the 1986 Tax Reform Act are still felt today and serve as a reminder of policymakers' enduring impact. These consequences are not only economic, but social programmes and public services are also affected, increasing the impact scale while making policy choices.

Besides that, within the post-Reagan era, economists have had to combine economic expansion with responsible spending. Sustainability is a core element concerning growing the economy, so there needs to be a balance between spending and achieving economic growth. This balance makes crafting policies extremely complex, requiring delicate trade-offs and sophisticated solutions to address conflicting priorities. We evaluate the international position of US debt, and American debt rests at the centre of the comparison. Other nations add value by showing what policies have been implemented in their debt management that makes them so different from America, enabling American policymakers to properly position America's fiscal policies worldwide. Going deeper focuses on long-term policy, especially the touted long-term policy and results indicators suggesting measuring the effectiveness of government policies. Without these numbers, making informed decisions becomes virtually impossible and more prudent legislation becomes elusive. In post-Reagan America, there is plenty to learn from the legacy that shaped social policies while also focusing on making bold moves on international policies. The legacy stands and says that America must exercise caution when fostering and helping new movements emerge today.

4

Wars, Bailouts, and Stimulus

Catalysts for Crisis

An Overview of Economic Catalysts: Defining Moments

Many impactful moments from past global economic periods tend to pivot around an economy-defining occurrence that constitutes history. Such moments lead to the development of national debt and other finances, as well as fiscally aggressive and responsive policies in a nation. They provide a better understanding of the development of a particular geopolitical event in juxtaposition to the state's economy. Further economic aid, for example, the acumen from militaristic activities worldwide, is essential for a government's financial stability. The linkage between expenditure related to conflict and the increasing debt a nation owes is rather profound. Waging war on a more profound scale takes up a lot of capital, and cash creates military burdens. History markers show how the cost of war rises and the taxes levied to cover this expenditure multiply, forcing them to seek substantial finance while also going deeper into deficit. Financing armed violence alongside post-violence socio-fundamental economic activities strengthens the reasoning for calibrating arms and expenses waged on warfare. Even further, the budget impact is only a fraction of the effect on the economy moving forward. Afterwards, it must spend years contemplating better revenue spending options over resource allocation. A study on these catalysts suggests that in moderating civilisation, the main machinery in amplifying arms redefining capabilities, for instance, is modernisation, which dominates cash for national debt encouragement.

We explore warfare's impact on fiscal policy and national debt monitoring through the lens of resource economies, attempting to capture every detail of the enduring marks left by conflict in history.

Military Conflicts and their Financial Toll

Wars have impacted the economy's pace and rhythm since time immemorial. The conducting of war is not only a military affair but touches the national budget, trade, inter-country finance, and even future policies. The direct impact of war includes spending on arms, logistics, and troop movements, as well as the indirect impact, which stretches for decades in the conflict-occupied nation and can cripple the economy and alter the allocation of funds needed for government services. War generally encourages the State to allocate finances on a broader scale, which will lead to tightening financing and increase the finances that have to be

THE DEBT TRAP 51

given away during later years, meaning tighter control will have to be exercised over these funds in the future. Military conflicts reduce the immediate state finances and affect several factors of the national economy, leading to stagnated growth.

Wars have an undeniable economic influence. This includes supporting veterans, re-establishing infrastructure, and addressing social disorder. Their healthcare, alongside rehabilitative needs and war pension systems, severely burden the economy. In addition, they represent an enormous financial cost to the nation. However, the greatest cost stems from human value. Marked by a lost surge of productivity caused by the redirection of civilian resources and capital towards wartime efforts, it becomes apparent that most attribute these redirecting funds toward mundane livelihood activities. An analysis of past conflicts highlights the profound cost of 'after' hostilities, making evident the necessity to consider the depth wage a country consents to in military action.

Furthermore, the chaotic aspect of armed conflict can have dire consequences on financial management and economic prognosis. The consequences of a conflict on the price of energy, exchange rates, market confidence, and overall economic activity can severely impact worldwide commerce and investment. War initiates an energy transformation, leading to changes in circulation for consumption and investment. The appropriation of resources toward productivity heightens and exponentially strengthens the military-industrial complex, resulting in changes that can affect consumption and capital-labour allocation. The relentless expenditure on military operations and activities requires a thoughtful review of enduring economic viability relative to funds allocated for defence and other equally important sectors like education, healthcare, and civil works.

Considering the above, citizens and policymakers must understand the intricate military conflict's economic impacts. The fiscal burden of conflict necessitates a holistic understanding of its public finance effects, national debt structure, and the wider economy. Applying these understandings to policies enables more reasoned and realistic responses to mitigate the adverse impacts of military action. When societies confront the challenges of enduring conflict, they strive to promote sustainable resilience, reinforcing the true costs of conflict on geostrategic factors. It is crucial that these responses are not just reasoned, but also practical and implementable, to effectively address the economic impacts of war.

The Long Shadow of the Iraq and Afghanistan Wars

The Iraq and Afghanistan wars have had a profound and enduring impact on the economy of the United States. The chronic conflict in these regions has consumed an exorbitant amount of financial resources. Even at the very beginning, the estimated costs related to the wars were astronomical due to the continuous deployment of troops, military assets, and even the construction of bases. Servicemen and women who paid the ultimate price in these endeavours will be remembered; however, the ongoing effects of these conflicts will be felt at multiple levels. The long-term healthcare expenses for veterans, along with disability and survivor benefits, further amplify the financial strains. The devastation of social and physical infrastructure in the affected areas requires extensive reconstruction efforts, which add even more expense to the total sum of costs already incurred. Coupled with the deficits in the federal budget, the ongoing conflicts in Iraq and Afghanistan impose a financial burden due to the diversion of funds from domestic spending and the renewals of priorities reallocating funds to serve external needs. Indirect wartime expenditures such as debt associated with spending also compound the federal military budget due to direct military spending.

The consequences of these interest payments extend to future budgets and further complicate national debt. The economic impact is long-lasting and evident as one considers the support needed for veterans, diplomatic activities, and aid offered to other countries. The conflicts highlight the intertwining factors, such as military activities and the economy, that shape laws and spending decisions long after the conflicts end.

Financial Bailouts: Necessity or Burden?

One of the most polarising debate topics in contemporary society encompasses the question of financial bailouts. The lack of consensus stems from whether the government should intervene during a financially difficult period. Supporters have a solid foundation in believing that providing aid is necessary; failing to do so will result in the complete disintegration of major institutions. Catastrophic events within the economy tend to have far-reaching shockwaves that will negatively impact the overall economy and greatly increase unemployment rates. This would lead to an uncontrollable population meltdown. Moreover, supporters also highlight the short-term costs of bailouts, which seem to be negligibly low compared to the consequences suffered in a systemic meltdown. Some critics oppose this, highlighting the "moral hazard" issue associated with bailouts. Markedly, company policies are shaped with the attitude of, "If we are going to bail you out, then you are free to put yourself in danger." This also consequently overshadows the main ideas of corporate discipline, ethics, and 'market' that have served as a basis for social order within a society or country. The scope of this study shall focus on the analysis of financial bailouts in detail by evaluating their effectiveness in preventing economic downturns and restoring the confidence of the markets. The 2008 financial crisis is worth closely examining concerning the epic failure of the bailouts that the public and policymakers deemed controversial. Also, examining government responsibility in oversight within the context of these bailouts is crucial for understanding the high-level implications of fiscal responsibility, trust, and confidence. In addition, the moral obligation of using public money to prop up failing businesses requires deep scrutiny, especially considering other societal needs that are often not prioritised. While attempting to understand the problems of financial crises and strategising how to resolve them, the need to analyse the implications of these bailouts becomes clear from a social, political, and economic perspective. It sheds light on how these burdens are woven into the very fabric of society.

The 2008 Financial Crisis and Government Intervention

The year 2008 witnessed the financial crisis popularly known as the Global Financial Crisis (GFC). It can be claimed that this event represents one of the most extreme turning points in the life of the market economy. Globally, there was a sharp decline in unemployment levels and a remarkable decrease in business and consumer confidence, which amplified the situation. Having its roots in the US housing market bubble's collapse, the crisis spread across the globe within no time. Businesses halted their operations, and several banking institutions failed across the globe. This placed governments in an unresolvable dilemma: how to curb the negative implications and prevent an overall collapse of the economy.

After the financial institutions suffered, almost all countries paved the way for a new approach to dealing with such situations. In the US, TARP (Troubled Asset Relief Program) was initiated, which aimed to safeguard the financial system from further damage by purchasing toxic assets and equity of stricken financial institutions. The government's intervention on such a large scale was intended mainly to restore liquidity in the credit markets, which were paralysed with fear and uncertainty.

At the same time, central banks engaged in aggressive monetary policies by setting interest rates at unprecedented lows and starting quantitative easing to increase liquidity to the banks. Furthermore, governments tried to deal with the underlying factors of the crisis by implementing reforms like the Dodd-Frank Wall Street Reform and Consumer Protection Act, which attempted to increase control and supervision over the financial sector.

Nonetheless, the effectiveness and equity of these actions were hotly contested. For example, many critics argued that the bailout money disproportionately went to large banks while smaller struggling homeowners and businesses did not receive adequate assistance. There was a growing public outrage alongside the discussion of moral hazard, executive remuneration, and the widening inequality gap within society, which emerged as a dominant political issue.

Moreover, the scope of these government interventions was beyond the domestic context, creating a unified response and policy action from international bodies like the International Monetary

Fund and the G20. This crisis illustrated how the global financial system is interlinked and the need for cross-national approaches to coping with systemic threats.

Regardless of the debates regarding these interventions, their impact cannot be ignored. The government provided a basis for minimal recovery after averting complete collapse and stabilising the financial system. However, the remnants of the crisis still serve as reminders of the impact a free market system and responsible government policies can have.

Fiscal Stimulus Packages: A Double-Edged Sword

Stimulus packages have been heralded for many years as one of the most effective tools to lift an economy out of recession and recuperate economic growth. However, the packages do have accompanying risks and issues. Thoughtfully designed stimulus measures can greatly improve the liquidity in an economy's financial system, increase consumer cash flow, and create investments for addressing economic gaps or 'missing pieces'. The very implementation of the package is its design, scope, and the overarching economic setting accompanying it.

One of the issues to consider with economic stimulus is the attempt by governments to control the level of spending on infrastructure or economic activities. Considerable amounts of stimulus funds tend to be circulated in the market; hence, inflation is a huge risk. There is a need for emergency capital while keeping a watchful eye on the set inflation rates. This leads to a healthy dose of financial industry decision-making and attention on the markets to see their responses.

Effective allocation of resources in fiscal stimulus packages demands meticulous planning and rigorous oversight. The return on investment in stimulating economic activity is found in capital projects, emerging technologies, and the development of existing and future workforce skills. However, this also necessitates unwavering vigilance to prevent the misuse of funds and ensure that the stimulus's purpose is not diluted through poor management, bribery, or misappropriation of taxpayers' money.

Most consider the sustainability and public finance consequences the main fiscal stimulus issue. While available financial support may be welcome, the public debt burden can restrict future generations and the government's ability to face unexpected challenges. Attempting to achieve an equilibrium between immediate action and maintenance of spending discipline is challenging and involves carefully planned trade-offs.

Lastly, taking too long to deliver fiscal stimulus is equally damaging, as waiting too long may deepen and lengthen an economic recession. Conversely, initiating an expenditure programme too soon, or using it too liberally to proactively address downturns brings the danger of market distortion, thus creating an unsustainable period of growth, also known as a post-expansion contraction.

When considering these nuances, fully utilising the possibilities offered by fiscal stimulus packages still requires comprehensive economic evaluations, careful risk-control strategies, and protective actions to defend long-term financial viability, balance, and stability. This competence is only possible through well-crafted policies with proper surveillance, enabling effective and sustained recovery from economic turmoil.

The Great Recession: Lessons Learned and Overlooked

Global economic history has been irreversibly altered by the Great Recession, which lasted from 2007-2009 and continues to impact financial policies and discussions. The recession highlighted the degree to which financial markets and economies worldwide are interlinked and the risks that come with deregulated financial instruments. Unavoidably, the recession taught lessons that significantly influenced future economic policies, but equally important are the recurring oversights that go unnoticed. The importance of regulation, oversight, and risk management established within the financial sector is one imperative lesson from the Great Recession. The financial crisis of this period was unprecedented. It was propelled by many opaque and complex financial products available due to insufficient regulations and unrestrained innovation. This period showcased the necessity for a wholesome regulatory approach, supervision encouraging innovation and dynamic shifts in the market, and risk prevention. Another lesson that can be learned from the Great Recession is the need to address inequality in wealth distribution to improve the economy. Stagnant wages and the unsustainable financial burden exacerbated household finances, which further deepened socio-economic divides.

How policymakers deal with the aftermath of a recession remains a key focus of research, particularly regarding creating and providing economic opportunities when there is a risk of over-leveraging an economy. A major lesson from the Great Recession is the growing need to rethink the policies of a central bank, considering the fiscal and monetary measures available. The degree of intervention with monetary policy and market controls during the last decade's recession had more stabilising impacts than any other crisis, generating significant controversy in its aftermath. Attempts to analyse past policy approaches to justify some restructuring were met with an understanding of the necessity for 'ex-post policy'—active policies to tackle unanticipated economic disruptions. Thus, the engaging narrative of a robust economic structure has been woven into the social fabric ever since the Great Recession, reflecting a relentless pursuit of greater resilience and adaptability, and presents a framework for versatile response-guiding policies around the globe.

Comparative Analysis: Precedents from Past Crises

The lessons learned from past economic crises are a treasure trove of knowledge. By building a case based on historical precedents, we can gain valuable insights into the policies, turning points, and other key highlights that have guided nations towards development during times of crisis. The Great Depression of the 1930s, the oil crises of the 1970s, and the dot-com bubble of the early 2000s serve as rich sources of information for studying methods of resolving economic turmoil.

The Great Depression, recognised as the longest and most severe downturn in a nation's economy, was characterised by unemployment, widespread national bank failures, and severe currency deflation. The implementation of public works programmes and the New Deal is said to have greatly influenced substantial economic intervention and introduced New Deal economics as the first adopted fiscal policy in the face of recession. During this time, borders were crossed with innovation, fostering Keynesianism as a prevailing ideology.

Similarly, the oil crises of the 1970s, which arose from geopolitical conflicts and supply disruptions, caused considerable upheaval in global markets and initiated stagflation. Countries faced the dual challenge of rising energy prices and stagnant growth, prompting a reconsideration of strategic partnerships and policies. The subsequent diversification of energy supply and conservation strategies were pragmatic responses to the vulnerabilities exposed during these crises.

The period around the turn of the millennium, when the dot-com bubble deflated, underscored the risks accompanying reckless speculation and unchecked market enthusiasm. The subsequent market correction highlighted the relationship between technological advancement, investment fervour, and regulation. Insights gleaned from this episode have shaped contemporary discussions on risk, market volatility, and the careful balance of innovation and risk within financial markets.

By examining these reference points, contemporary policymakers and economists can better understand how previous interventions and strategic adjustments have been crafted to mitigate the impact of modern crises. By reflecting on the multifaceted nature of past crises, societies can identify underlying themes, structural weaknesses, and resilient aspects that have historically guided economies through turbulent times. This analysis fosters a deeper understanding of the complexities of crisis management while challenging prevailing notions often regarded as self-evident in economic policymaking.

Contemporary Case Studies: COVID-19 and Beyond

The COVID-19 pandemic marked the onset of a uniquely volatile period for economic activities. It required a revision on how public expenditure policies are designed relative to national debt and posed existential questions on how debt was being accumulated. The handling of the pandemic by governments all over the globe prompted extremely contractionary spending policies that were instead meant for economic upswings. These policies certainly conflicted with prior spending and borrowing clauses set and managed by the state, drastically affecting the economy in the long run. Macroeconomy and public finance are systematically analysed in this section regarding the spillover effects of various economic stabilising policies during the pandemic-induced recession period through direct fiscal relief packages. The assistance provided globally during the pandemic serves as a great real-time example to understand the impact of expenditure schemes on healthcare, public finance, and industry bailouts. In light of this, public policy is studied critically through various lenses to analyse the effectiveness (or lack thereof) of the pandemic-induced fiscal hurdles in different states. With this perspective, the chapter examines the policies developed during the pandemic to understand potential improvements to the resilience of expenditure policies borne out of crises. While traversing forward from the pandemic, this section seeks to chart a trajectory for state expenditure, alongside contemplating the potential consequences of the debt on national finance strategically and geopolitically.

Focusing on recalibrating the fiscal policy frameworks following the COVID-19 pandemic, the discourse pays attention to debt reduction strategies, budgetary allocation sustainability, and even prospective reforms to enhance economic fortitude. While depicting contemporary case studies shaped by the pandemic and planning for the future, this section provides a guiding context on public debt management strategy development to aid policymakers and other interested parties in navigating the complex and evolving global public debt landscape.

As pandemic-related shocks drastically disrupt the economy's pre-existing equilibrium state, there is a need to analyse public finances in exceptional detail and focus on what rebalancing implants sustain growth in the medium-term horizon (usually three to five years). Economists often label this period the post-pandemic phase.

Balancing Act: Future Considerations for Policy Makers

Exploring pandemic shocks, one must try to analyse the sharp rises in public expenditures as part of coping mechanisms adopted by states to mitigate the impact of the pandemic. This is no small feat for the discerning policy analyst. Deciding which factors to prioritise when crafting policies aimed at driving economic growth while at the same time curtailing rampant inflation calls for scrutiny from every possible angle. Understanding the obstacles instead of attempts at solutions put forth reveals what can foster meaningful, constructive debate.

Shifts in global trade and sustainable development tend to have an underlying premise that revolves around a perpetual balance of risk and reward. Historically, the world has witnessed a systematic approach to danger, neglecting economic connectivity.

Carrying forward this logical fallacy, policy responds to the danger, diacritically omitting integration and interaction paradox, in combination with climate change, presents a conceivable risk for policymakers not keen on adopting carbon-inclusive tendencies to lessen the impact of industrial activities.

Essentially, this not only seizes the opportunity as an ethical obligation towards the environmental domain but also nurtures prospects focused on investing in innovation while allowing green shelters, which are constructions free from aesthetic logic fences civilisations wall in.

Lastly, other topics require urgent attention devoid of disparity and social welfare, unleashing issues alongside constructive action based on inequality. Focused solutions aim to create and facilitate policies fortifying social borders while sadly beyond monumentally harming disparity.

Alongside these, enablement opens up educational shields, strengthens state-aided healthcare, prepares the citizenry, and nurtures a driven workforce that, in forecasted scenarios, emerges resilient and loaded with endurance alongside the rest being plunged into eventuality imbalance.

At the same time, restrictions make trust in accepting democracy futile in emerging digitally triggered frameworks. In the backdrop, nurturing the citizens by ethically sponsoring change facilitates the range in scope of emerging mundane actions revolving around technology.

As a primary concern in fostering a functioning economy, a policymaker must deal with complex and often clashing priorities and stakeholder demands. With the right and informed leadership decisions, after considering consultation with stakeholders, nations will have the potential to achieve prosperity, cohesion, and sustainability. Creating cross-sectional policies incorporating and balancing economic, socio-cultural, and environmental concerns gives rise to responsible and anticipative governance. After all, the effects of wise policy-making decisions are a matter that shall live on for many years and continue to impact the socio-economic landscape of the future and sustain a thriving society for generations to come.

5

Political Polarisation and the Debt Ceiling Debacle

Introductory remarks on political polarisation.

In the last few decades, political polarisation in the US has intensified unprecedentedly and significantly altered legislative operations and policy spending effectiveness. The pronounced ideological divide among the political factions has made it impossible for the government to function or govern, contributing to stalemates and political gridlocks that adversely impact fiscal policy-making. In examining the growth of political polarisation, it is clear that the development towards hyper-partisanship has occurred through a slow but steady process influenced by socio-economic and cultural events and factors throughout history. To appreciate these intricacies, it is essential to explore the history and evolution of the partisan divides that have given rise to the state of political polarisation witnessed today. The genesis of political polarisation can be linked to the sociocultural transformations in the second half of the twentieth century. The civil rights movement, the Vietnam War, and the feminist movement, among others, fundamentally transformed American society and created new political dividing lines that increasingly defined American politics. These divisions became even more pronounced with the rise of cable television, social media, and other digital communications that offered platforms for selective exposure to differing political opinions, thus broadening the gaps between opposing ideologies. These conditions have contributed to the polarisation of political culture, making compromise and cross-party agreement increasingly hard to achieve.

The impact of deep political divides is observable in public finance policy as well as public policy. The political conflict between the parties has stalled important fiscal policies, resulting in budgeting problems, shutdowns, and an altogether hostile attitude toward public debt and deficits. Therefore, their ability to execute sensible fiscal policies and undertake strategic economic initiatives has been greatly impaired. In addition, finding consensus has been replaced by legislating from the edge, whereby self-serving political games come first instead of serving the people. As a direct consequence of politics being so divided, compromise has become harder and is addressed only in terms of spending on infrastructural issues, which oversimplifies complex problems. Grasping how deeply divisive partisanship is, in the context of how few politically motivated policies are, ipso facto means attempts to understand how far apart the poles are, which is critical to understanding the impact political division has on effective governance and economic policy. After studying its past and pondering its consequences, it is hoped that such a vision will be possible for the fracture in governance aimed at building national welfare.

Historical Context: The Development of Partisan Division

Partisan tensions have been one of the most determining factors throughout the history of the United States, both politically and economically. This evolution dates back to the beginnings of the republic, as the first divergent visions for the future of the nation became manifest. The debates between Federalists and Anti-federalists regarding the ratification of the Constitution began to establish the first political camps in this country, already prone to sharply marked divisions on an ideological level that would later become emblematic of the politics in this country. Territorial expansion and the industrial rise of the nation continually created new fractures, leading to the formation of the Whig and Democratic parties. The Civil War subsequently reinforced regional and ideological disparities as well as the confrontation between Republicans and Democrats as we know them today.

The association between conservative and progressive ideas in the early part of the 20th century led to significant changes, as evidenced by the New Deal and the Civil Rights Movement – two major milestones in the emergence of partisan modernism. The cultural and social upheavals of this period in the United States during the 60s and 70s ushered in a new era with as much division as intensity surrounding issues of civil rights, women's rights, and the Vietnam War.

The rapid development of cable news and internet services pro-
liferated the use of echo chambers and partisan rhetoric, increasing
suspicion between political parties.

Reviewing the past reveals the repetitive conflicts of politics sep-
arated by phases of relative amity, collaboration, and unity against
angry deadlocks. The evolution of these divides has shaped the
trajectory of domestic policies as well as America's standing in
the international community. The constant tensions of bipartisan
unity and conflict have severely impacted policies dealing with
economic spending, fiscal responsibility, and national debt. This
history in itself is important in understanding modern-day politically charged polarisation and its effect on crucial matters, such as
the debt ceiling clash and debates.

The Dynamics of Political Leverage: The Debt Ceiling

As a part of the financial architecture of the United States, the debt
ceiling has received extensive scrutiny as a political weapon, forcing
ideological conflicts, extreme partisan confrontations along the
lines of the 'doomsday' mental stance, and even alleged factional
blackmailing. Like all issues subjected to intense nationwide debate and controversy, the mechanics involved in lifting or simply
'suspending' a ceiling is an intricate system of economy-wide re-
verberating procedures and implications.

The ceiling may be approached as an arbitrary 'hot' threshold
to which a gap sets forth rises, and the accumulation of possible debt to be paid in the form of fixed government spending
increases. The sum of the so-called static balance horizontal and
drawing resources along the vertical axis form an axis that will

always circle an equilibrium, lend its hand, and encircle and logically spiral outwards. Without exceeding the ceiling in the shape of an open-ended box, towards which a cap set approaches the finite perimeter on the graph. Failing to lift the lid may lead to calamitous outcomes such as financial bankruptcy appearing on a global scale inevitability emerging suspension of would rotationally propel terminating causally identified cycle along the horizon resolve guarantees invested from ruinous obliteration big bang steamrolling crashing conflict paradoxically on inner rings, or level crashing harbours embarking on credit spiralling intimidate. This oscillating cycle makes tirelessly struggle deep down to populate, navigate, sculpt, and meticulously carve out policymakers' breath resolve under rational fiscal scrutiny to ensure smooth whirlwinds see glance balanced economy 'always ensure stability'.

In reality, discussions about the debt ceiling are often blended with ideological conflict on the scope of government, spending, and even relevant issues of the nation. They tend to require extensive bargaining, intricate legislative strategies, and sophisticated political manoeuvring as both parties of the political divide try to exploit the problem to serve their purposes. The consequences of such a political spectacle, with its great drama and dramatic potential, reveal the sociopolitical impacts that the debt ceiling poses on governance and the trust of the public.

In addition, using the debt ceiling as a bargaining tool creates risk and instability in economic markets, impacting investment confidence and even broad national productivity. Periodic stand-offs regarding the debt ceiling have caused disruptions in government operations, payment defaults, increases in market instability, and increased volatility that pose serious threats to the stability of the US and global economies.

Thus, the overall picture around the debt ceiling shows considerations beyond just the techno-bureaucratic and structural sides formed by the strategies of stakeholders, the requirements of powerful economies, and the interests of society. To appreciate the finer details of this particular lever of finance, explaining the intricacies of American politics requires analysing global power relations one step further.

Case Study: Government Shutdowns and Brinkmanship

Government shutdowns serve as a hallmark of political brinkmanship concerning the debt ceiling. These extremes demonstrate the unfortunate realities of partisan gridlock where critical services are not supported due to bipartisan budget disagreements. The most notable example of a government shutdown in recent memory was when the United States government was shut down from December 22, 2018, to January 25, 2019, which spanned a record-setting 35 days. This shutdown came into place as a result of a contentious debate that was politically motivated, owing to a disagreement over a border wall. Such face-offs not only paralyse the federal government but also have a rampant negative impact on the economy as a whole by creating high levels of uncertainty and economic disruption. Prolonged shifts in government employee work schedules cause financial stress, both personally and professionally, for those with government contracts due to the payment delays, project halts, and service interruptions that result from later start dates. Moreover, such shifts in government work hours result in a loss of trust among citizens regarding the self-governance capability of their leaders, negatively impact confidence in institutions, and cause an erosion of the nation's international status as a symbol of stability and governance. Furthermore, such work schedule disruptions increase the chances of uncertainty within the financial sector, which can alter the overall perception of economic growth and other accounting metrics.

Looking at it broadly, the occurrence and consequences of government shutdowns pose certain issues regarding the enforcement of fiscal restraint and the wisdom of governance. The real and human suffering and the systemic impacts of these self-inflicted crises call for action on underlying causes that make political standoffs and brinkmanship possible. Budgetary politics, partisanship, and the debt ceiling are situations that our country is encountering that require a reassessment of the way this nation is governed, its culture of politics, and its systems.

Main Actors: Lobbyists, Congress and the Presidency

Within the folds of the governance-mandate-implementing policy prism, main actors are known to influence critical decision outcomes and bureaucratic policy change responsibly. As the legislative body of the United States, Congress has a significant role in formulating and passing the budget, spending, and even voting on the debt limit. The internal organisation of Congress itself, comprised of the House and the Senate, with each member representing different constituents, gives Congress so many competing ideals, making its decision-making highly subject to partisan politics and factional infighting.

At the same time, the presidency has considerable power relating to the policies of finances and budgetary issues. The president sets the tone of the economy, either through enforcing discipline with budget gaps or through the submission of budgetary proposals and exercising the veto on bills. The relationship of the head of state with the parliament becomes especially important in cases when the government wants to fix the debt limit because, in both situations, there is a need to make political trade-offs to get an agreement.

Lobbyists who represent interest groups, businesses, and even advocacy groups strongly affect policy at the federal government level. These interest groups seek to influence the political sphere with their money and put forth their preferred legislation, which makes governance in the domain of finances much more difficult. Politicians, lobbyists, and constituents constitute a sort of triad that puts intense pressure on the decision-making process, which may cause spokespeople from different factions to enter into fierce confrontations.

Gaining insight into the case study surrounding the debt ceiling debacle requires an understanding of the motivations, pressures, and roles of various system actors. In this unfolding story, the existing and emerging dynamics of relations and conflicts of interest will create further opportunities and challenges for governance to find balance in policy frameworks and achieve lasting stability.

Media Influence: Public Opinion and Partisan Narratives

The media plays a pivotal role in shaping public opinion and influencing partisan narratives surrounding the national debt issue. With its power to amplify certain viewpoints and control the narrative, the media significantly impacts the public's understanding of fiscal policy and governance. Political polarisation has led to the rise of news outlets and media platforms catering to specific ideological leanings, further deepening the divide in how the debt issue is portrayed and perceived. In the realm of 24-hour news cycles and digital media, sensationalism often takes precedence over nuanced analysis, perpetuating existing biases and polarising viewpoints. This dynamic not only hampers productive discourse but also undermines the public's ability to critically engage with the complexities of fiscal policy. Partisan narratives are reinforced through selective reporting, cherry-picked data, and the amplification of extreme viewpoints, creating echo chambers that reinforce preexisting beliefs while marginalising opposing perspectives. Moreover, the media's framing of the debt ceiling debacle and its portrayal of political actors shape public perception and set the stage for potential policy outcomes. Biased reporting can lead to misinformed citizenry and hinder constructive dialogue essential for finding viable solutions. The media's role as a gatekeeper of information places a responsibility on journalists and news organisations to present balanced and factual coverage. In an era rife with misinformation and disinformation, the need for responsible journalism is not just paramount, but urgent. Understanding the intricate ways in which media influences public opinion necessitates a critical evaluation of media literacy and consumer habits. Consumers must actively seek out diverse sources of news and information, cross-examine claims, and critically assess the underlying biases in media narratives. Addressing the influence of media on public opinion involves fostering a more discerning and informed citizenry capable of navigating the complex landscape of fiscal policy and governance. Ultimately, the media's influence on public opinion and partisan narratives surrounding the national debt has profound implications for the democratic process and the formulation of sound economic policy. Recognising the media's

role as a conduit for public discourse underscores the imperative
for ethical and balanced journalism that fosters informed civic
engagement and transcends partisan divides.

Impacts on Fiscal Policy and Governance

The political polarisation surrounding the debt ceiling debacle has significantly impacted fiscal policy and governance in the
United States. As partisanship intensifies, the ability to form
consensus on crucial budgetary matters diminishes, leading to a
heightened risk of fiscal instability. This gridlock often results in
short-term funding solutions and temporary measures, under-
mining the government's capacity to make proactive, long-term
fiscal decisions. Moreover, the absence of bipartisan cooperation
undermines overall governance and erodes public trust in the government's ability to manage economic affairs effectively. The perpetual cycle of partisan fiscal battles creates uncertainty for businesses and investors as they struggle to anticipate the direction of
government policy. This uncertainty can deter investment, stifle
economic growth, and impede long-term planning. The failure
to reach timely agreements on fiscal matters has also affected the
functioning of essential government services and agencies, leading
to disruptions and inefficiencies. The organisational strain arising
from frequent debates and delays in budget approvals can hinder the effective delivery of public services, adversely impacting
citizens across the nation. Furthermore, the prolonged stalemates
and brinkmanship associated with addressing the debt ceiling and
related fiscal issues have implications for the country's creditwor-
thiness and financial stability. Heightened uncertainty in the wake
of recurring fiscal crises increases the risk of credit rating down-
grades, constraining the government's borrowing capabilities and

potentially elevating borrowing costs. These developments have far-reaching repercussions on the broader economy, including higher interest rates, reduced business confidence, and tightened access to capital for households and enterprises. Additionally, the erosion of fiscal discipline amid the heightened political bickering over the debt ceiling perpetuates an unsustainable trajectory for the national debt, posing long-term risks to the country's fiscal health. As decision-making lurches from one crisis to another, comprehensive and strategic fiscal planning becomes increasingly elusive, potentially jeopardising the nation's economic prospects and burdening future generations with the consequences of accumulated debts. In sum, political polarisation and relentless discord surrounding fiscal governance reverberates throughout the economic landscape, affecting fiscal sustainability, government functionality, and overall economic stability. Addressing these challenges necessitates a concerted effort to bridge the partisan divide and cultivate a more constructive approach to fiscal policy and governance. Bipartisan cooperation is not just desirable, but essential for economic stability.

International Perspectives and Reactions

The issue of US debt and its impact on the global economy is a significant concern for international actors, each with their own perspectives and reactions. The interconnected nature of the world's economies means that substantial shifts in the US fiscal landscape reverberate across borders, prompting responses from foreign governments, financial markets, and international organisations. Many countries closely monitor the US debt situation due to the dollar's status as the world's primary reserve currency. Any signs of instability in US fiscal policy can trigger concerns about the value of the dollar and global economic stability. As a result, foreign central banks and sovereign wealth funds may adjust their holdings ofUS Treasury securities, impacting interest rates and capital flows. Major trading partners such as China and the European Union have a vested interest in the health of theUS economy, as it directly affects their export markets and overall trade balances. Their perspectives onUS debt are shaped not only by economic considerations but also by geopolitical dynamics and strategic relations. International financial institutions like the International Monetary Fund (IMF) and the World Bank play a pivotal role in assessing the implications ofUS debt on the wider global financial system. They often provide analysis and recommendations aimed at safeguarding global financial stability amid shiftingUS fiscal conditions. The reactions of these institutions can influence market sentiments and investor confidence. TheUS debt's international repercussions extend beyond economic realms, as they intersect with geopolitical dynamics and diplomatic relations. In some cases, foreign governments leverageUS fiscal challenges to advance their own geopolitical agendas or negotiate strategic partnerships. At the same time, they must navigate the complexities of interdependence, recognising that excessive turmoil in theUS economy could pose risks to their own economic well-being. Overall, the varied international perspectives and reactions toUS debt underscore the complex web of interdependence among global economies and the interconnected nature of contemporary fiscal and monetary systems.

Resolution Attempts and Legislative Proposals

In the face of mounting national debt and political polarisation, policymakers have sought to address the challenges through various resolution attempts and legislative proposals. One approach involves revisiting the budgetary process to introduce more effective fiscal controls and long-term planning. This includes considerations for implementing balanced budget amendments or automatic stabilisers that could counteract the impact of economic downturns on the federal deficit. Additionally, there has been increased focus on exploring reforms to the tax code, such as closing loopholes and adjusting tax rates for higher income brackets, to generate additional revenue to curtail deficits. Furthermore, discussions have centred on the necessity of comprehensive entitlement reform. Policymakers have grappled with ensuring the sustainability of social safety nets while addressing their contribution to the overall debt burden. This has prompted debates over raising the eligibility age for specific programs, means-testing benefits, and recalibrating cost-of-living adjustments to better align with shifting economic conditions. Another critical aspect of resolution attempts involves efforts to streamline government operations and enhance efficiency. Proposals have included leveraging technology to modernise public service delivery, consolidating redundant programs, and scrutinising discretionary spending to identify areas for potential reductions.

Furthermore, there has been advocacy for greater transparency and accountability in budget reporting to foster public trust and oversight. Legislative initiatives have also aimed to address the debt ceiling conundrum more proactively and pragmatically. This includes exploring mechanisms to delink political wrangling from the debt limit approval process, whether by establishing automatic debt ceiling revisions tied to specific economic indicators or crafting bipartisan agreements that set predetermined borrowing limits. Moreover, reflections on past fiscal crises have spurred conversations about the need for a more coherent framework for crisis management. This encompasses the development of contingency plans, crisis response protocols, and enhanced coordination between fiscal authorities and central banking institutions to mitigate the impact of future shocks on the national debt and financial stability. Ultimately, the intricacies of resolving the debt quandary call for a comprehensive and multifaceted approach that navigates the complexities of partisan divides, economic realities, and long-term sustainability. As stakeholders continue to deliberate on viable solutions, weighing the trade-offs, considering historical lessons, and fostering a spirit of pragmatism to chart a sustainable path forward for economic stability is imperative.

A Path Forward: Bridging the Divide for Economic Stability

As we navigate the complex web of political polarisation and its impact on the debt ceiling dilemma, it becomes increasingly clear that a viable path forward must be forged to ensure economic stability. Bridging the gaping ideological chasm calls for a nuanced approach that transcends partisan lines and places the nation's fiscal well-being at the forefront. In this pivotal endeavour, policymakers, thought leaders and citizens must recalibrate their perspectives, prioritising rational discourse and pragmatic solutions over dogmatic stances and brinkmanship. A critical foundation for progress lies in fostering an environment where bipartisan collaboration is not merely an afterthought but a fundamental principle guiding governance. This can be achieved through comprehensive reforms to dismantle the systemic barriers that perpetuate gridlock and enable short-term wins at the expense of long-term fiscal soundness. It is imperative to shift the narrative from 'us versus them' to 'us for a stable future'. Drawing from historical precedents, it's evident that moments of profound national crisis have often served as catalysts for unity and transformative change. Embracing this ethos, stakeholders across the political spectrum must engage in constructive dialogue, elevating the common good above narrow interests and electoral calculus. Initiatives encouraging transparency, accountability, and evidence-based policy-making can foster a climate conducive to building consensus and enacting sustainable fiscal measures.

Furthermore, cultivating public understanding and participation is indispensable in fortifying the democratic process and empowering informed decision-making. By aligning the vision for economic stability with the values shared by all Americans, we can dismantle the barriers obstructing progress and usher in a new era of responsible governance. To this end, harnessing the collective wisdom from diverse perspectives can chart a course toward fiscal responsibility, safeguarding the nation's economic future for generations to come. The journey toward bridging the ideological chasm may be arduous, but the dividends of a stable, thriving economy are immeasurable and vital for ensuring enduring prosperity.

6

Economic Consequences

Interest Rates and Budget Strain

Opening Remarks on the Effects of Economics

The effects for a deaf nation on the economic imbalance of supply and money come from the government revenue and monetary decisions taken earlier, which either positively or negatively affect the nation's economy and finances. Regarding dealing with the complex trade systems of a country, a country's decision is dead to permeate its purchasing power on the health of all industries. The economy demonstrates complex interactions such as supreme banking policies and changes in price practice policies alongside a systematic modern economics complex branch of economics which studies the behaviour of money, including inflation, debt and other factors. Important for the welfare of the economy, which means the wealth of a nation, is based on dynamic economic facts; the interest is considered as the heart or measure of how finely an economy is doing, whether swimming or sinking. Adequate attention to interest rates clarifies customer spending determinants that account for economic activities such as investment undertaken, IOUs, and economic engagements, such as actively engaging with business lending while numerous others are busy. These activities affect the national economy. As a result, government issues will not only condition the nation's economy but also face the reality of economic needs for growth, which achieve the effect of being strongly funded and working throughout the wheels; not aligned leads to other differences, including a reduction in budgetary policies which creates gaps along with the budget.

Delving into the public debt domain, we uncover its fundamental economic implications: inflation, monetary policy, and public confidence. By reviewing historical cases and global examples, we underscore the importance of proactive intervention in policies that respond to economic realities. As we navigate the economy's fallout, it becomes clear that the multi-faceted nature of financial action and its reactionary response framework is of peak concern. This realisation engages decision-makers, intellectuals, and economy participants on an international scale, making them feel responsible for the economic outcomes.

Understanding the Economic Terrain of Interest Rates

Among the numerous factors affecting a country's debt, interest rates are extremely important because they can impact a nation in many ways. Navigating the economic terrain of interest rates requires the interaction of monetary policy, market forces, government borrowing, and policy guidelines, all working in tandem. As discussed earlier, central interest rates have a great deal of control over the spending level of consumers and public investment, as well as the country's debt level. Reducing the interest rate will allow governments to borrow more money since it will be cheaper, encouraging economic activities through public spending, investment in infrastructure improvements and other activities. At the same time, a reduction in the interest rate can hamper economic growth and increase the cost associated with debt servicing and private sector investment. As described earlier, the need to control and sustain other areas of the economy makes this a balance of sorts. The task of central banks is made even more difficult considering the need to achieve certain targets, making interest modulation and controlling other parameters of the economy harder to manage fluidly with growth targets. The economy in discussion has to be steered deftly about interest rates, inflation expectations, and legislation to control the country's unemployment level.

Moreover, the global interconnectedness underscores the urgency of tracking international interest rate developments. Capital movement and exchange rate relationships can amplify the effect of domestic interest rate policies, making it crucial for policymakers, financial institutions, and active participants to be proactive and prepared to deal with changes in interest rate trends. The impact of constantly changing technology, the financial marketplace, and political relations further accentuates the need for quick action to reduce risk and take advantage of such situations. This emphasis on urgency makes the need for immediate action to reduce risk and take advantage of opportunities clear to the audience.

Inflationary Pressure and Debt System

Increasing a country's national debt increases the likelihood that inflation will rise. Continuously borrowing to finance government activities and commitments will increase the total money supply in circulation. This increase in the money supply, known as 'currency excess', can create an aggrandised desire for available goods and services, resulting in price rises and inflation. In addition, the increased level of public debt will likely diminish available resources and the confidence of stakeholders who will perceive the economy's sustained growth as a cause for a substantial inflation risk.

Inflation's impact can compound the national debt. When prices increase, the effective value of debt diminishes, alleviating the repayment stress on the government. Nonetheless, this risk creates enormous price uncertainty, where the future value of money is uncertain, that could distort investment and planning at both the business and individual levels, leading to distorted economic resource allocation and decision-making.

Moreover, inflation's effects are not limited to the country's borders. Inconsistent inflation can also drive up the outflow of capital from the nation as it deters foreign investors from buying into UK debt securities and trusting UK currency, worsening the inflation cycle. Furthermore, fixed-income recipients, pensioners, and even savers are affected as their inflating spending power gets eroded, reducing the level of financial security that can be sustained.

Resolving the challenges posed by the combination of debt dynamics and inflation requires a comprehensive approach. This approach should incorporate prudent fiscal policies, coordinated monetary policies, and policy frameworks. It should also involve reining in expenditures while directing most of the spending towards fostering economic recovery to greater levels. Controlling the increase in debt with increased spending requires proactive monetary tools that manage liquidity and interest rates. Stronger, clearer communication policies are essential in improving the confidence held in the economy and reducing the uncertainty invested parties face. This stress on the need for a comprehensive approach makes the audience feel the gravity of the situation and the need for a well-thought-out strategy.

Diverse historical examples have made it clear that managing debt and inflation is a delicate balance. However, an attempt to manage or mitigate the consequences of an excessive accumulation of debt and inflation depends not only on the amount of debt but also on its dynamics, which in turn requires the cooperation of all members of society and policymakers.

Fiscal Deficits: Impacts In The Short And Long Run

Whether fiscal deficits are short-term or long-term, they impact the economy. In the short term, they can help stimulate growth and productivity during recession and stagnation. Deficits can increase aggregate demand through capital spending, inciting greater spending and investment. While this resurgence is favourable, great caution about inflation, debt, or any other is necessary. On the other hand, reoccurring and sustained fiscal deficits tend to have a broader range of effects and limit prospects for future economic growth. The 'crowding out' effect is the primary concern, whereby excessive government spending increases borrowing, limits private investment, and stunts innovation and productivity.

Throughout spending, however, the growth of deficits is uncontainable and can set off a chain reaction around the economy, which is detrimental.

Additionally, soaring deficits lead to higher interest rates, resulting in negative effects on the financial sector and ultimately increasing the cost of servicing debt. This cycle of destruction can block potential growth and vitality in the economy and limit the government's effectiveness in unexpected emergencies. Increasing the deficit leads to an imbalance in fiscal policies, raising concerns for specific groups who rely on government support. Even further, in regards to 'generational equity', the growing burden of repaying debt is too often laid at the feet of future taxpayers, limiting opportunities and greatly harming their well-being.

Moreover, continuous deficits might erode investor confidence and lead to capital flight, a weakening currency, and the currency's depreciation, impacting international trade and overall economic competitiveness. Prudent management of the economy, including specific policy actions, strategic resource distribution, and long-term budgeting discipline, is required to lessen these consequences. Fostering a precarious equilibrium of capitalising on short-term relief from inflation while guarding against long-term harm remains a significant challenge for decision-makers and economists. With deep analytic capabilities, the intricate issues regarding fiscal deficits create opportunities to enhance the prosperity and resilience of the economy.

Budget Strain: Understanding Scope and Scale

The budget-estimating process strains the government and the entire public sector; budgetary restraints give rise to challenges throughout any nation. In any given society, comprehending the budgetary constraints on revenue and expenses is a prerequisite for understanding the healthcare system and its economic determinants. In a nutshell, while estimating the budgetary strains, one ought to ascertain not just the arithmetic addition or subtraction but the more severe social consequences like changes in public services, the level of available investment, and the health of the economy. Considering the consequences of budgetary strain, factors like demographic changes such as ageing, changes in age distribution, shifts in welfare requirements for the elderly, as well as how taxpayers perceive their social acceptance attempt to change public spending. These changes, along with presumably positive (or neutral) changes like an emerging population through immigration, control the basic changes to claim old age pensions dominating citizens' expectations, enabling public policy to flexibly limit the age at which citizens can expect to receive a pension, creating a definable need. Alongside identifying a range of public spending programmes, a combination of requirements enables resources to define spending principles for allocation; eco-societal constraints require effective allocation to foster sustained growth as responsive societies face allocation that directly leads to fostering equity, respite on socio-political order, and erodes welfare.

Regardless, analysing the budget strain scope requires quantitative and qualitative approaches. In addition to public debt, the quality of public spending and likely returns on such investments are important indicators of budget strain. In addition, proactive steps to increase revenue or optimise expenditure frameworks become fundamental in reducing budget strain. For example, rationalising tax policy, reducing subsidised expenditures, and controlling wasteful expenditures can alleviate fiscal strain. Addressing the extent of budget strain requires knowledge of systems within an economy and the foresight to other emerging issues.

Zhanga has underscored the lack of understanding of these complex ambiguities as the reason policymakers and citizens cannot use these straightforward principles. With an understanding of these deeply rooted phenomena, everyone should be free to shape informed plans to resolve budgetary stress and support enduring fiscal well-being.

Challenges and Responses to Monetary Policy

The staggering national debt presents a complex economic landscape, with one critical aspect demanding immediate attention-its impact on monetary policy. As governments strive to steer the economy towards growth and manage fiscal stress, the central banks find themselves at the forefront of mitigating the effects of escalating debt levels. Monetary policy, traditionally aimed at managing the money supply and interest rates to achieve price stability, maximum employment, and sustainable economic growth, now faces the intricate challenge of providing necessary economic stimulus while addressing concerns about unchecked inflation and financial system instability.

Central banks play a pivotal role in managing fiscal stress, primarily through interest rate management. By adjusting short-term interest rates, they influence the cost of borrowing for consumers and businesses, thereby impacting investment, consumption, and economic activity. However, this task becomes more challenging in the context of mounting government debt. Lowering interest rates can reduce the debt servicing cost, but it may also lead to increased inflationary pressure and asset price inflation.

On the other hand, raising interest rates increases the cost of servicing the government's existing debt, thus further straining public finances. In addition, this may lead to a fall in investment and consumption, which could weaken the economy's growth. Therefore, it can be observed that central banks face profound challenges when constructing a monetary policy to address a rising national debt.

Another way to respond to monetary policy is by incorporating unconventional approaches like quantitative easing (QE) and forward guidance. After the onset of a financial crisis, many economies experience dormant growth for a prolonged time, thereby forcing central banks to undertake QE programmes to increase the financial system's liquidity by purchasing financial assets and decreasing the interest rate on lending for an extended period. These strategies might also assist in reducing the burden of government debt through diminished borrowing costs; however, there can be equally troublesome implications in other areas, such as financial markets and the real economy.

Furthermore, the central banks must craft clear and concise messages for the market and the public. These messages serve as a guide, helping stakeholders understand the plan of action. Clear instructions are key in expectation management and settlement for any actions taken due to monetary policies. However, dealing with the economic impacts of excess debt brings forth the struggle of central banks attempting to be open while flexible enough to promptly accommodate changes in the economic environment.

In trying to overcome this problem, there is a need for close monitoring of various economic dimensions, including but not limited to, the rate of inflation, unemployment, the general growth of the economy, and the activity in the financial markets. There is also an increase in emphasis on collaboration with the fiscal body, since the interaction between the two policies determines the growth of debt and its effects on the national economy. Through all these efforts, central banks try to enable economies to cope with the underlying complications of hoping to minimise budget deficits. At the same time maximise long-term sustainable growth. This collaboration is not just a necessity, but a shared responsibility towards the economic stability of the nation.

Reactions from the Private Sector

A nation's ever-expanding government debt and fiscal policies have a direct correlation to the private sector. During economic stress, private companies deal with consequences that must be addressed across many sectors. While there are numerous implications, one of the most vital is how government borrowing affects interest rates. A significant amount of a country's debt will most likely result in higher rates, thus increasing the cost of business loans. As a result, lenders may become more restrictive, which decreases the investment capacity of the private sector and hinders economic growth. Increased uncertainty concerning future taxation policy, as well as the sustainability of public finances, prompts cautious behaviour towards expansion and new investments. Many changes in the landscape of public debt can shift the confidence level and behaviour of consumers, impacting the demand for goods and services and the sales for different firms. It is more difficult for companies to devise plans concerning allocating capital, managing risks, or strategising amid enduring concerns for heightened competitiveness and financial resilience. As businesses face these challenges, multi-year planning has become an international concern due to the swift changes to global and national debts. The efforts from the government to manage fiscal deficits drive foundational changes in policies and regulations, which causes private sector companies to shift how they manage and allocate these vital resources.

Moreover, the private industry is directly connected to government expenditures and their allocation to infrastructural projects, healthcare services, and education. Changes in government spending can have far-reaching effects on diverse economic sectors, affecting the extent of contracts, revenues, and overall market conditions. Firms in the strategically sensitive tranche of servicing government contracts tend to adapt to changing funding priorities if they choose to accept government aid. Also, contracting grant government cuts potentially require added attention from the private sector. Under these constraints, the self-governing sector is responsible for the government's support policy, engaging with decision-makers concerning economic policies needed for development that support the economy's growth. Coordination between state and private sectors becomes necessary to solve all those problems with the negative value created by the increasing state debt. Positive commentary and open dialogue are helpful tools private entrepreneurship can use to create effective discipline, order, and governance without suffering economically. By sponsoring responsible policies, fair fiscal management, and effective risk control, they can evade the challenges brought about by governmental debts and discretionary spending.

Government Spending Prioritisation Problems

Shifting the focus to government expenditure, the process of prioritisation is often multifaceted, as it requires deliberatively intricate critical thinking and choice. Since funds are always limited, policymakers often find it difficult to decide how to optimally distribute money to achieve maximum benefit to society amidst competing needs. In addition to the competing demands, there is a publicly available need for spending such as national security, infrastructure development, healthcare, education, and social welfare programmes.

The prioritisation of government spending problems is one challenge that balances spending on immediate and long-term benefits. While short-term needs such as disaster relief and stimulus packages grab headlines, allocating resources to education and research funding is essential, as well as an investment in long-term sustainable projects. Thus, balancing short-term needs and long-term social development is almost always extremely demanding.

In addition, fairness and equity are considered in discussions surrounding government spending. It is especially challenging to balance helping economically depressed groups and encouraging growth. The allocation of resources across sectors and populations indicates a society's value systems and priorities. This makes fairness and equitable allocation a significant element of the prioritisation problem.

The balance between government spending and the economy's stability also adds a layer of nuance to the prioritisation problem. There is a need to balance controlling spending to reduce the possibility of a recession and sustainably managing fiscal resources. Not addressing budgetary stress, such as identifying overspending sinks, can damage the increasing national debt, interest rates, and ability to remain financially stable.

The shifting pace of technological development and societal problems resolves the puzzle of government spending in a different light. Effectively allocating funds to solve emerging problems like cybersecurity, adapting to climate change, or developing new medical technologies requires strategy and innovation.

Ultimately, dealing with the prioritisation challenges within the context of government spending requires advanced reasoning, stakeholder involvement, and an open approach to the decision-making process. While striving to achieve balance, governments must attempt to unlock the full potential of resource allocation to meet core societal needs by actively engaging in quality dialogues and insights with experts and citizens.

Draw Historical Lessons From Historical Cases

Various nations have encountered critical debt crises, providing a greater understanding of national debt. These historical parallels help make comparisons that can help overcome current policy-making and strategic challenges. One such primary example is the 1980s Latin America debt crisis, which stemmed from uncontrolled governmental spending incurred by excessive borrowing. This case serves as a reminder of the extreme financial burden. Restructuring the debt and providing international support can also be seen as measures to overcome such crises.

Another example is Japan's severe deflationary depression and heightened public spending following the asset price bubble in the early 90s. This illustrates the long-lasting effects of the public debt burden and the obstacles associated with managing it. Moreover, the Greek case during the European sovereign debt crisis highlights the dangers of high debt levels in a monetary union. It demonstrates the relationship between economic integration and the sustainability of the regional financial system.

Additionally, studying the post-World War II reconstruction processes in devastated countries such as Germany aids in understanding the complexities and prospects of rebuilding an economy burdened by debt. The reconstruction policies of Germany and other nations provide modern policymakers with insights into the impact of increasing national debt on economic growth, invest-

ment, and public welfare. These case studies also underscore the
need for responsibility in fiscal spending, the promotion of national development, timely interventions, and economic reforms
to mitigate the adverse consequences of excessive debt. By inter-
weaving the lessons from these historical events with contemporary economic issues, decision-makers can better create sound
plans to manage the growing national debt and reduce its impacts.
Post-analysis of debt crises reveals that some of the primary lines of
action needed to sustain national economies are proactive strategies, solid governance, and coalitions without borders, as these
factors enhance the resilience of economies during adverse shocks.

Conclusion and Preparing for Future Challenges

The analysis of the economic consequences of interest rates and
the associated budget strain demonstrates that proactive measures
are necessary to confront future challenges. The value of studying
historical examples cannot be overstated. These case studies have
provided important lessons for policymakers, financial specialists,
and the public, identifying potential abrupt turns, maladaptive
strategies, and promising paths forward. Whether within more
complex and uncertain frameworks, an essential landscape of responsibility and sustainability envelopes every looming fiscal glut-
tonous predation and negative externalities.

One striking feature is the need for comprehensive, coherent,
and integrated approaches that blend short-term strategies with
long-range commitments. This includes careful management of
inflationary forces, the impact of interest rates, and the interplay
between fiscal deficits and monetary sovereignty. Relieving budget
strain requires many approaches, including slowed spending and
strategically smart prioritisation, frugal resource allocation, and

strict accountability safeguards at the systemic, institutional, and governmental echelons.

The bewildering amount of difficulty that lies ahead demonstrates the need for clearer choices and preparation. Policies that react to change quickly, as well as new economic models, are needed to keep up with global innovation and technological changes. Society can be better prepared against collapse by fostering responsible and advanced financial skills through education.

Moreover, response measures taken by the government and reactions led by the private sector merit parallel analysis due to their direct impacts on the private financial crisis. Strengthening economic policies is essential in assuring that planned initiatives do not have a detrimental long-term impact on stability and growth, thereby making the enhancement of public-private cooperation one of the priorities. A high level of trust is essential for forming healthy relations that stimulate optimal policy-making and responsible governance.

One of the necessities these policies should meet is the focus on learning from the world's history alongside forward-focused thinking. Balancing past practices with modern inventions leads us to adaptive resilience, steering clear of the danger zones of stagnancy and narrow-mindedness. By gaining insight from past experience, there is an opportunity to gain strategic foresight to strengthen the efforts needed to enhance our society.

Ultimately, the end of our exploration highlights the intertwined connection of history, modernity, and futurism in crafting economic futures. By reflecting individually or in groups and committing to implementing tangible steps, it is possible to go beyond uncertainty and achieve long-term economic stability. Preparedness for emerging challenges is directly proportional to the ability to integrate information, cultivate new ideas, and establish strong leadership principles that ensure prosperity for the future.

7
Global
Implications
US Debt on the World Stage

Conceptualising the Global Financial Networks

Transactions, investments, and policies work hand in hand to form the backbone of the modern economy, and the intertwined global financial networks are intricate in nature. This magnificent system encompasses banking institutions, stock markets, commodity exchanges, and trade on an international level. Understanding the interconnectedness of these financial networks enables learners to comprehend the aftershocks of US debt within a global context.

At the heart of these systems lies a concept of interdependence - the core idea behind these global networks. International trade revolves around the health of various nations, which have far-reaching impacts on others. Relief and spending on a country's economy endanger the balance marked out by other nations and force them to spend more. The impact of US debt is felt beyond borders as it will affect politics, financial markets, currency values, stock bonds, interest, and the confidence of entire societies.

Furthermore, these financial networks do not only limit themselves to the private sector, but they also include government and supranational institutions. The central bank in the given country, regulatory frameworks, and international organisations shape the overall parenthesis of these networks while maintaining them. Their frameworks aid and help sustain system policies set forth, which serve as the boundaries for panic arising from neutral funds in debt.

The mobilisation of capital for investment, hedging, or risk management crossing territorial boundaries relies on sophisticated networks, which require an in-depth understanding of various financial tools and mechanisms. These include, but are not limited to, derivatives, instruments of the sovereign debt market, and even securities. While they enable free-flowing trade, underlying vulnerabilities expose participants to potential systemic contagion effects.

Technological innovations in the digital age increasingly integrate global financial networks, allowing immediate transactions and information sharing. Technological advancements such as high-frequency trading, algorithmic risk management, and the introduction of digital currencies have changed the landscape of international finance and brought challenges and opportunities.

Analysis of US debt on an international scale gives insights into the global financial network. It reveals the myriad ways foreign economies impact the United States due to America's international debt. Such analysis affords an understanding that serves as a basis for subsequent exploration of the impact of international trade on the financial system's economy.

The American Dollar as the World's Reserve Currency

The world's primary reserve currency is the US dollar, which has been at the centre of international commerce, trade, finance, and investment for years. This makes life easier for the US and helps its economy wield substantial global power. Countries across the globe keep large reserves of US dollars in their central banks and governments, allowing them to trade internationally more easily and stabilise their own currency. The prominence of the US dollar further intensifies due to its use in calculating the price of oil and other global market commodities. The United States is at the front of the line in setting international trade policies, directing them as it wishes. It can exercise significant control over international monetary decisions, shape trade policy, or address strategic international relations concerns. Unfortunately, this leads to some risks. Economies that are more developed and emerging are affected when the US dollar is detached from the other currencies. The sensitive nature and host of risks attached to the dollar increase casualties due to falling reserve currency value, US market economic policy changes, and value shifts.

A loss of confidence in the stability of the US dollar may cause significant financial destabilisation as countries and institutions scramble for new ways to conduct international trade and manage their finances. Therefore, the overriding importance of the US dollar continues to draw attention and argument in light of the shifting global economic order and emerging centres of competing currencies. In light of these considerations, the implications of the US dollar's status as the reserve currency for the world are crucial in understanding the complex web of the international financial system and the problem of dealing with the growing US debt.

Trade Imbalances and Their Impact on Debt

On a more technical note, a trade imbalance occurs when a country's imports of goods and services exceed exports, creating a deficit in the balance of trade. This creates negative problems within the country itself, alongside the negative effect of debt imbalance in economic spending on an international scale. As a result, one of the main issues arising from trade imbalance is the heavy reliance on foreign-controlled funds to finance both consumption and investments. Due to this fact, persistent trade imbalance tends to put regions that have a chronic trade deficit under some kind of foreign aid umbrella, turning their economy into a subsidised one and increasing its susceptibility to external shocks. As per the effects of trade imbalance, currency values become more unstable and fluctuate, causing countries to forcefully reduce the value of their own currency compared to other countries to boost export value and improve trade. These problems also go beyond the economic sphere, as one country may find its trade with its partners unbeneficial, thus leading to quarrels over trade, which may result in trade wars and reactive acts, resulting in further deteriorating effects on the economy at an international level. From the debt standpoint, persistent trade imbalance aggravates a country's debt burden by continuously financing domestic consumption out of foreign-generated funds. Furthermore, scarcity of locally produced goods and services may also cause locally produced wages for such services to stagnate. Combined with income inequality, this creates a high chance of workforce redundancy or economically inactive citizens.

Trade imbalances must be dealt with nationally and internationally using policies that enhance export competitiveness, reduce imports, and encourage trade. International agreements and cooperation can also mitigate the causes of these trade imbalances while fostering enduring economic development worldwide. Regarding the debt of the United States and its global impact, strategically addressing trade discrepancies is important for constructing a more stable and durable world economy.

The Impact of the American Fiscal Policies on Global Markets

The impact of US fiscal policy on international markets is quite remarkable since the actions of the US government determine the conditions and the financial stability of the world economy. One of the largest factors that affect international markets is the US government's budget deficit. A large budget deficit usually tends to increase spending, which increases borrowing in an economy and leads to a growth in interest rates. This means that the cost of borrowing increases, and with an adverse economic situation, investment and overall economic growth in many countries suffers. Moreover, US fiscal policies, encompassing taxation and public expenditure, can profoundly affect international commerce. Tariffs, subsidies, and other kinds of trade policies executed by the United States can disturb global supply chains and create shifts in the market for several industries worldwide. In addition, the US dollar, being the world's primary reserve currency, vastly increases America's control and the impact its policies have around the globe. Changes in monetary policy and stimulus spending by the federal government cause swings in exchange rates and the price of currencies, disrupting and blocking investment capital streams worldwide. In addition, the decisions taken by American authorities related to finance and credit changes may introduce dreadful imbalances in the global economy.

For example, the slightest sign of a change to the US economic policy may cause a surge of volatility within the market and uncertainty for investors, thus having dire consequences on the international equity and bond markets. Due to the nature of a globalised world, any movements made on the US fiscal policies tend to have an instantaneous impact on the international community, which trickles down from stock valuations to even sovereign debt yield rates. Therefore, it becomes imperative to track the movements of the US policy and its subsequent impacts on the global stage for policymakers, investors, and businesses operating internationally.

Debt Dynamics in Emerging Economies

Emerging economies are of great importance in the international financial system, and as they begin to emerge as global players, providing additional services or goods to the world strengthens the company's position; understanding their debt dynamics is vital to understanding the acute impact that US spending-fuelled debt has on the world. These economies encounter some of the most important issues managing their debt, such as exposure to exogenous shocks, volatile currency, and restricted spending capacity. Additionally, the debt's intricate structure, comprising both internal and external elements, further complicates the analysis of their debt dynamics.

One of the primary elements of debt dynamics in emerging economies is the interaction between the debt and its ratio to the economy's growth. The economy is susceptible to high debt because scarce resources would be allocated to non-productive public investments instead of capital expenditure, leading to lowered productivity and economic growth. Moreover, over-reliance on foreign debt exposes these economies to severe risks during currency depreciation and global financial instability.

Public debt management in emerging economies tends to be correlated with monetary policy, exchange rates, fiscal control, and the imbalance in financial discipline. Crowding out private investment by lending to the government increases the cost of borrowing, creating high interest rates that negatively disrupt economic performance. Therefore, managing sustainability becomes especially important in these contexts, owing to the need for financing and the dangers of debt distress and defaults.

Also, integrating emerging economies into the global economy increases the spillover effects caused by changes in debt in the United States. These changes have powerful consequences for the cost and availability of debt financing, the overall economic outlook of these countries, changes in capital markets, interest rates globally, and investor sentiment. Hence, the stability of the design of the international financial system and the control of debt issued by the US become crucial for the survival of these new markets.

It is critical to note how multilateral institutions and international cooperation deal with emerging economies' debt issues. Collaborative action through social policy on sustainable debts, financial aid, and policy execution promotes synergy and reduces emerging economies' vulnerabilities. Moreover, debates on reconstructive governance issues like transparency regulate an emerging market's financial resilience and ability to stabilise the global economy.

The world is grappling with increasing US debt, and emerging markets are already struggling for some level of economic independence. Understanding the fundamentals of debt issues for emerging economies is critical because this set of problems is a double-edged sword. The growth of an economy, sustainability of debts, international finance, and multinational partnerships all intricately coexist while confronting issues emerging on multiple fronts of the growing debts in emerging economies.

The Effects of United States Debt on Investment

Changes in US debt are likely to have palpable effects on international capital investment due to its systemic influence on the economy. The United States is one of the largest economies and, therefore, holds critical importance. Debt levels are one of the most stark factors affecting the attitude of both domestic and foreign multinational corporations (MNCs). Debt is often considered a double-edged sword - on the one hand, debt increases the fiscal expenditure of the economy, improving growth, easing interest rates, and incurring higher levels of sustainable debt. At some point, severe debt levels begin to pose issues around repayment alongside putative growth levels.

Additionally, changes to debt per se and related policies will alter the balance of payments and flows in currency markets, directly impacting the dollar's value and thereby changing foreign perceptions of US assets. Multifaceted phenomena relating to the value of the dollar, foreign investment, and assets shape capital investment around the world, thus impacting markets and the conditions of world economies. For example, cyclical fiscal developments influencing the economy, such as spending, will prompt responsive changes to financial assets, resulting in the outflow of assets from the economy. This cycle of events will intensify volatility globally, leading to some nations facing uncontrolled expenditure restrictions. In general, ameliorating the plight of debt, due attention enhances investor pre-emption, leading to growth and enabling capital inflows, thus fortifying markets.

Furthermore, the character of international capital movements is influenced by the magnitude of US debt and how appealing other countries are for investment purposes. Therefore, while attempting to resolve the debt issue, the US must maintain a favourable and secure environment for investments to continue attracting foreign capital. Policymakers and market players actively monitor these investments due to the highly globalised structure of economies and the plausible impacts arising from variations in US debt value. Ultimately, strategically directing the effects of US debt on international capital investment is essential to ensure sustainable economic development and fortify global financial stability.

The Role of Multinational Organisations in Debt Management

The growing interrelation of economies worldwide requires the attention of multinational organisations, especially regarding sovereign debt management. Entities within this group, including the International Monetary Fund (IMF), World Bank, and regional development banks, have far-reaching influence on countries' fiscal security and economic development. Their financial assistance, technical support, and policy recommendations aim to address the challenges posed by excessive debt and promote scenarios for enhanced growth through sustainable pathways. They alleviate the burden of economic distress by providing resources and guidance necessary to modify the fiscal policies of nations with structural adjustment policies, debt relief programmes, capacity-building initiatives, and other forms. Support in debt management from multinational organisations extends beyond the provision of funds and includes advocacy for increased transparency, accountability, and governance reforms. They also provide access to international markets, allowing negotiations between debtor countries and international creditors for favourable terms for debt sustainability and economic recovery. The combined action of the government, business community, civil societies, and other stakeholders actively engaged in debt issues exemplifies a multidisciplinary approach to comprehensively address the problem from all angles rather than focusing on a single aspect. All these efforts assist in examining the debt problems with a holistic perspective. This illustrates how different countries, regions, and people are interconnected and reliant on each other and demonstrates the structure of the world financial system.

Furthermore, these institutions undertake careful evaluations and monitoring to assess the effectiveness of debt management plans, recognition of potential risks, and best practices fostering long-term economic strength. Using their skills and power in unison, multinational institutions try to deal with the sophisticated debt management system and, in the process, guard sustainable development and financial strength across the globe.

Geopolitical Considerations and Diplomacy

Geopolitical considerations and diplomacy are fundamental to US debt management within an international context. The relations of world powers and regions interrelate with international organisations and influence the approaches used to solve the constantly increasing debt problem. While the United States is dealing with its financial difficulties, the complex web of geopolitical relations begins to emerge and dominate, deciding the focus of attention for tactical measures and strategic plans to be taken in the long run.

Diplomatic attempts to lessen the negative effects of US debt go beyond the usual bilateral relations between the countries. G7 and G20 summits serve as examples whereby the world's economic powers have a forum to talk and collaborate for mutual benefit. These diplomatic settings become highly important in trying to reach an agreement on how to resolve economic and debt imbalance at a time when action and responsibility are needed.

Economically and regarding security and strategy, geopolitical factors are of primary concern and do not require further explanation. Defence pacts and military alliances with the United States highly rely on the perceived stability and sustainability of the US economy along with global security initiatives. This means that debt management has more varied implications than just economic policies, which need to be dealt with at the very least at the level of sophisticated strategic international relations.

The United States is strategically ahead of its peers in considering international politics, as they can integrate diplomacy to showcase themselves as committing to back spending and growing the economy, which includes the entire globe, sustainably. Especially in the developing world, those extensive financial negotiations need to be managed along with encouraging economic growth to decrease reliance on aid and funding while simultaneously controlling debt, showcasing the dualism between diplomacy and financial responsibility.

In terms of diplomacy, the strategic correspondence differentiating bilateral and multilateral needs further emphasis. Strategic alliances and negotiations frame the circumstances within which the US debt is viewed. Diplomatic avenues offer pathways to contentious and sensitive trade and investment relationships, along with financial policies that shape the perception of global investors, which subsequently impacts their investment decisions.

Furthermore, bilateral engagements are the least analysed but arguably the most impactful. Their role critically shapes the investment confidence of global market participants and international observers. Proactive planning in global relations is crucial for managing US debt in an international context.

Global Collaboration: Addressing The Debt Dilemma In Unison

Due to the rising US debt issues, a collaborative strategy is required to resolve it because US debt has global ramifications, given the international integration of global finance. The debt poses challenges for international economics, which underlines the need to tackle this problem with concerted efforts. Cooperative actions should focus not only on managing the effects of US debt but also on long-term planning to avert risks in the future. The most striking element of this cooperation is that no nation can solve the debt puzzle using its methods. To address such an urgent economic problem, the multidimensional approaches of various nations are essential. In addition, cooperation fosters the emergence of a new order based on transparency and responsibility, enabling enduring engagement for deals and shifts in the act. Also, countries need to act concertedly to enhance the US's capability to manage debt by jointly strengthening the infrastructure internationally. Another vital area is to create a common floor concerning regulations and governance that would protect the international financial system by rendering it more united and covered against shocks.

Further, developing a common understanding of global economic interrelations is critical for formulating policies and strategies to manage and alleviate the effects of US debt. This effort requires nations to be willing to talk, engage, and constructively interact toward a common vision of addressing existing economic problems. Building a culture of cooperation also means using the resources of international and other multilateral organisations to encourage joint action. Nations can work together over long periods to address the complexities of US debt from a coordinated approach so that policy actions are balanced, comprehensive, and reflect different national interests and focuses. Besides coupling policies for coordination, collaboration at the global level creates new possibilities for cooperation that are not restricted to economic cooperation but also include strategic, diplomatic, and geopolitical cooperation. Coming together to solve the debt problem gives nations the opportunity to establish strong partnerships to ensure long-term economic stability and growth. There is no doubt that tackling the problem of US debt from a collaborative perspective is one of the most powerful ways to create a global economy that is fair, equitable, and stable.

Conclusion: Strategic Approach for Future Interactions

Managing the inevitable global debt requires a strategic perspective for future actions. The modern economy is overly integrated, making finding solutions to the issues of US debt in international

relations overly complex. It is important to note that no country can combat the consequences of increasing debt in isolation.
Therefore, a strategically focused framework on international relations is needed that emphasises collaboration and countermea-
sures.

An important element of the strategy includes alleviating restrictions on international negotiations and alliances. Creating
forums for stakeholders to address public debt issues along with
monetary and trade policies is also important. Participating in
open negotiations enables nations to analyse one another's issues
and arrive at workable solutions. The processes aim to craft coordinated responses to restore stability in the global financial system
and counter the impacts of growing debt.

In addition, focusing on emerging markets and investment opportunities requires a strategy that looks ahead towards sustainable economic development. With the US debt burden having
cross-border repercussions, strengthening infrastructure, widening the scope of responsible lending, and increasing access to financial services in developing countries becomes essential. This
advanced approach aids in global stability while fostering inclusive
opportunities for growth and development in communities left
behind due to imbalances in spending policies.

Besides, a rethinking approach concerning the role of multinational institutions in debt management is important to the strategic approach. Multidisciplinary approaches to debt relief and reconstruction, capacity strengthening, and technical assistance can
be developed in collaboration with the International Monetary
Fund (IMF), World Bank, and other regional development banks.
When these institutions offer their expertise and resources, this
brings form to the tangled realities of the global debt system.

Moreover, the advanced strategy requires that nations reset their diplomacy and geopolitical thinking against the backdrop of escalating financial credit burdens. The responsibility of diplomacy is fundamental to the creation and maintenance of economic peace and the prevention of wars resulting from economic stress. While pursuing international relations, countries are likely to expect that such relations will assist in creating favourable conditions for collaborative actions towards resolving the debt problem, stabilising markets, and strengthening the economy.

As stated in the previous remark, diplomacy has wide-ranging, foresighted, anticipatory consequences for any planned action. Adopted by the world's virtually sole superpower, it poses the most complex and, arguably, pressing problems for any country intending to develop in a world increasingly dominated by American debt, stimulating the emergence of a new balanced order.

8

Policy Proposals

Addressing a Growing Dilemma

Overview of the Policy Framework

Marrying the debt problem with current economic issues reveals an endless stream of competing frameworks and ideologies for policymakers to contend with. The core issue of spending, taxing, and growing a nation remains among the discussions. One framework that seems to answer is that of a balanced budget which dictates that all spending must equate to revenue, emphasising the need for long-term fiscal sustainability. This approach, with its emphasis on responsibility and oversight, provides a reassuring structure to prevent runaway deficit spending, unchecked debt, or borrowing.

On the other hand, critics argue that government expenditures have the highest potential for developing stronger economies if they aren't forced to comply with the balanced budget model. Commitment to such a model might also restrict powerful public welfare and social programs if deemed too generous. This shows the other side of the diabolical face of aggressive fiscal discipline, where the focus needs to be on bringing about positive, sustainable economic growth.

Furthermore, other policies like Keynesian economics focus on counter-cyclical spending, which is essentially increasing government spending during economic downturns to stimulate the economy. This is done to relieve a recession and assist aggregate demand. Supporters believe that planned deficit spending during a slump can jump-start the economy and result in job growth, thus improving the long-term fiscal situation. However, opponents warn of the dangers of excessive reliance on deficits, particularly the possible inflation, crowding out of private investment, and increasing interest payments on the country's debt.

Also, some supply-side economic theories, which focus on reducing taxes and regulations to stimulate productivity and encourage entrepreneurial activities, assuming that strong economic growth will help close any budget gaps. Nonetheless, others argue that this approach invites greater income inequality, lesser revenue, and deepens structural deficits.

This debate on these crucial policy positions highlights the blend of politics, economics, and public finance. Therefore, assessing each option's advantages and disadvantages and their real-world effects is necessary in responsibly balancing priorities against the nation's long-term economic health.

Overspending Can Also Be Managed Using A Balanced Budget Method

Eliminating the gap between revenue and spending should be a goal for each government, as this would help them mitigate national debt. Maintaining a balanced budget guarantees a check on spending and income to ensure the government does not go into deficit. Achieving this goal leads to a consequent decrease in the government's borrowing, thereby reducing the debt. A balanced budget policy demands a total review of the current programs and services; it does not mean cutting spending on crucial services and programs. Instead, it entails rethinking the taxation structure and other revenue-generating activities to increase income while contributing to economic growth. Alongside these, efforts toward a balanced budget make it essential to conservative forecasting in long-term commitments, ensuring sufficient sustainable resources. Upholding this policy requires firm alignment beyond political considerations, manifesting in a bipartisan endorsement of prudent spending, which shows the government's management level. These are some of the benefits of a balanced approach. Additionally, a balanced approach increases confidence domestically and internationally, showing the government as responsible managers of taxpayers' wealth.

Following this method can improve the nation's economic stability and governance climate, all of which will improve citizens' welfare. In conclusion, adopting a balanced budget approach is one of the most effective ways to resolve the current fiscal problem and sets a strong foundation for achieving a better economy.

Tax Reform: New Boundaries for Earning Revenue

Addressing the tax reform problem is perhaps one of the most important elements in relieving the national debt and developing sound economic policies. When the government attempts to relieve budgetary constraints and try to boost the economy, one of the first policies to consider is usually a change in the tax policy. A well-planned and executed tax reform has the potential to significantly improve the economic landscape, offering hope for a more prosperous future.

Following the public debate on changes to Beia's tax system, policymakers must develop new approaches to amending the tax code. This involves simplifying, closing redundant loopholes, and removing outdated mandates that give undue chances for tax avoidance or evasion. Besides, adopting progressive taxation, where high-income earners proportionately shoulder a larger share of the burden, is also socially friendly and aims at giving equity and welfare value redistribution. In addition, using technology and digitalisation in tax administration can improve processes, increase compliance, reduce fraud, and enhance the fundamental strength of the tax system.

Adopting these measures to strengthen the general environment for initiating and carrying on business activity through specific grants and entrepreneurial credits may result in increased economic activity and broad-based prosperity. In addition, corporate taxation needs to be approached with a clear strategy that seeks to balance international competitiveness and public contribution. This comes alongside the consideration of international taxation, which has to be dealt with alongside globalisation in a systematic way for cross-border transactions and multi-national operations.

Any proposed changes to the tax system will not be successful without assessing the potential impacts they would have on revenues and the economy. Taxes and revenues, by nature, come with constraints, and, as a result, policies require comprehensive analysis and simulation to study the effects of different reform options. This rigorous approach to decision-making instills confidence in the fairness and sustainability of the tax system.

Good tax reform should be accompanied by a stimulus to improve the sustainability of public finance. This would ensure that the government functions and meets its responsibilities while creating a space for the economy to thrive and encouraging business opportunities. With more flexible and bold approaches, policymakers can build a modern tax system that is adaptive in meeting the demands of today's socio-economic realities.

Spending Priorities: Assessing and Redefining National Needs

When tackling the ever-growing challenges of public debt, it is critical that a thorough assessment of national spending priorities is done. This step requires an analysis of government expenditures and potential reorganisation towards other areas. Through this evaluation of national issues, policymakers will formulate coherent policies considering budget allocation, resource management, and expenditure to achieve sustained economic growth.

An example of this would be allocating more funds to primary care practices to improve health outcomes in a population or taking a systematic approach to managing resources that ensures efficient service delivery. The shift from supporting activities to focusing on outcomes contributes to aid effectiveness; therefore, by setting priorities and enabling spending disciplines, the government adds value to its fiscal policies. Understanding emerging challenges in the healthcare system or the need for new models or paradigms of health systems.

It also involves an analysis of social behaviours, innovations, and socio-technology changes. The changes in the population movement and age of the people are of particular importance. This set of dynamics on a requirements basis requires a vision and ingenuity for strategic planning of the resources. Newer methods in medicine will change what needs to be spent on research healthcare facilities and infrastructure for medicine. Social changes in demographics will also necessitate changes to social security and welfare services.

This also entails considering issues relating to renewable sources of energy. This will make it possible to consider great matters of nurturing the environment while benefiting public spending policies economically. Government spending needs to purposely shift focus spending policies while seeking to balance development and encourage the heightened utilisation of protective measures.

Ultimately, evaluating and updating the national requirements is more than just an expenditure; it is a diabolical plan that guides national development. It requires a sophisticated grasp of socio-economic interplay, attention to detail on new developments, and strong foresight. With prudent decision-making, policymakers can create a plan that improves spending, increases social welfare, and strengthens the economy for a long time.

Debt Relief Approaches: Immediate and Extended Strategies

The reduction of the national debt encompasses a variety of blended approaches that encompass both long-term and short-term strategies. In many cases, addressing the issue requires a blend of spending minimisation, revenue enhancement, and temporary budgetary measures. In the case of these short-term approaches, they stand to lessen existing pressures on the budget or avert further debt accumulation, although not for extended periods. That said, short-term interventions often come with trade-offs. While short-term relief is necessary through these economic interventions, implementing policies, especially those focused on austerity, tends to be counterproductive, which strengthens the imbalances within the system. The existing social inequities can further hamper this goal. Thus, the need to ease funding restrictions imposed on social programmes becomes essential.

While short-term policies appear to mask the cracks, extended measures are proving far more effective—such as aggressive structural reforms to social programmes, devising an umbrella policy on taxation, effective investment within the country's infrastructure, and enhancing its skilled labour force. Addressing these problems enables lower and more balanced national debt numbers by compensating where natural debt levels may be reached.

Bipartisan cooperation, strategic foresight, and a commitment to hard spending are essential for achieving meaningful long-term solutions. Moreover, these strategies will ensure that reductions in long-term debt accounting plans will calculate shifts in population characteristics, changing socio-economic factors, and global integration. Integrating both short-term requirements and long-term goals is critical for establishing a sustainable framework for responsibility in debt and finances. Adopting an encompassing approach for short and long-term initiatives addresses current fiscal hurdles and helps lay a solid financial framework for coming generations. While navigating challenges related to debt reduction, using a blend of immediate short-term measures will support maintaining economic stability over the long run. This policy will help safeguard the well-being of the economy and the country.

Monetary Policy: The Federal Reserve's Role in Debt Management

By implementing monetary policy, the Federal Reserve System (Fed), with its expertise in foreseeing and controlling broad factors such as the money supply, credit, interest rates, and inflation, plays a crucial role in the nation's debt management. In managing the money supply and the availability of credit, the Fed sets interest rates and controls inflation. In this part, we will focus on how precisely the Fed balances the different aspects of debt management.

To start with, it would be helpful to consider how the Fed's modulation of the economy influences the actions and processes of the governmental bodies. The Fed can either raise or reduce its key interest rate, which may enable or obstruct borrowing, investment, and economic activities. Favourable financial market conditions significantly impact the government's capacity to refinance its debt. We will also showcase the ripple effects of the Fed rate change on bonds, investor trust, monetary policy, and debt dynamics.

Additionally, the Federal Reserve's financial operations encompass the buying and selling of government securities, which helps manage funds and short-term interest rates. This part of the paper will show in detail how such transactions affect the amount of money in circulation, the availability of credit, and the yield curve, thus affecting the level of borrowing and debt servicing by the government.

One more important detail worth noting is that the Federal Reserve is the last resort lender in the case of a financial crisis. Through the provider's credit and emergency loan services, the central bank can reduce systemic risk and assist some financial institutions, which might lead to the disruption of the government securities market. This provider's (of last resort) function regarding the management of direct public debt will be interrogated in depth.

In addition, this part will examine the Federal Reserve's actions concerning monetary policy execution—its communication policy and transparency. The clarity and decisiveness with which the Fed takes action have profound effects on the markets, especially bond yields and the government's borrowing costs. The impact of the Fed's forward guidance and sustainability on long-term debt will be scrutinised.

Finally, the possible issues and constraints about the Federal Reserve's role in managing economic debt will be analysed. The issues surrounding the central bank's independence, the limits of control, and the voluntary trade-offs of balancing financial stability and price equilibrium will be analysed, revealing the deeper issues of harmonising monetary policy with responsible debt control mechanisms.

Bipartisan Collaboration: Overcoming Political Partisanship

Amid rising political polarisation, there is a growing concern for bipartisan solutions to the national debt problem. The constant clash of Democratic and Republican ideologies underscores the need for both parties to work together, often stalled by party politics. However, historical examples of bipartisanship working towards fiscal responsibility prove it is possible to manage debt. An analysis of former attempts such as the Social Security reform of 1983, the Balanced Budget Act of 1997, and the COVID-19 relief funding reveals that progress can, and has, been achieved through bipartisan efforts. These solutions focused on central economic principles of controlled spending, revenue collection, and multi-year debt alleviation, which served as the foundation of effective negotiation. Progress necessitates fostering an atmosphere of compromise and debate, no matter what competing ideologies dominate the discourse on the ever-growing debt problem. This approach will allow both parties to address the fundamental differences in accepting all opinions from both sides in reconciliation, offering a beacon of hope for the future.

Moreover, promoting higher transparency and responsibility in allocating public resources can enhance public confidence and compel political representatives to seek deeper long-term fiscal sustainability policy objectives for the nation rather than shallow short-term political gain. To encourage bipartisan agreement, establishing bipartisan task forces or commissions that focus on comprehensive strategies for debt alleviation could create an environment that nurtures constructive participation. By focusing on the commonly defined objectives of the nation's economic well-being and future development, bipartisan actions can go beyond political inclinations and foster innovative, pragmatic policies directed toward solving the issues related to national debt. Nevertheless, adopting a spirit of understanding and working together across different parties is the most effective way to deal with political stalemates and create a sustainable roadmap toward fiscal responsibility for the United States.

Legislative Tools: Powers and Limitations in Debt Control

The country's legislative tools concerning debt management are fundamental in determining its economic direction. In this part, I will explain the spectrum of the available actions that combine the powers and limitations of legislative attempts to tackle the ever-increasing challenge of the national debt.

One of the most important instruments available to the legislature is the authority to impose fiscal policy, which includes budgeting and public spending. Congress exercises control over budgeting by approving each federal budget and allocating it to different programmes and agencies. In this way, lawmakers can guide the total government spending and, in turn, the speed at which the country goes into debt.

However, the usefulness of legislative aids is not without restriction. Political gridlock, differing party ideologies, and complicated rules and procedures inhibit control and the enforcement of debt control policies from being put into action swiftly. The checks and balances meant to exist within the legislative system can enable endless discussions and deliberations that could have otherwise been dealt with quickly, thus creating a delay when the action taken does not match the needs of the economy.

Also, there is a debt ceiling, which is considered a legislative limit set by Congress on the total amount of money that the US Treasury can borrow. However, the debate on the periodic increase of this limit serves as a bone of contention, adding volatility to the financial markets and reducing confidence in the government's ability to pay back its obligations.

Furthermore, the complex relationship between the executive and legislative branches adds further nuance to controlling debt. The president's veto power and control over policy priorities create an active tug-and-pull in crafting fiscal decisions, even when Congress controls the nation's finances.

As a final point, comprehensively analysing the overarching context of existing authoritative delimitations within legislative procedures reveals the most pertinent aspects necessary for effectively addressing national debt challenges. Proactively working to alleviate national debt within the constraints of legislative frameworks allows policymakers to balance responsible governance with political realities, setting the stage for long-term economic growth.

International Models: Adopting Lessons From Global Counterparts

With technological advances, the world is more connected than ever. In this global framework, countries need to move from domestic policies and actively learn from each other to solve economic concerns. A key example could be the pandemic's effect on a country's national debt; one can learn much by studying international frameworks. As the world becomes more interconnected, there is a need to learn how other countries deal with the same financial issues to broaden a policymaker's scope of solutions. Policies relating to international learning must consider the differences in cultures within countries. For example, some countries have dealt with deficit spending and high borrowing levels, while others have concentrated on investments and economic growth. These nations have addressed fiscal irresponsibility by allocating stimulus packages. Both approaches have unique advantages and disadvantages, which must be fully understood to make an informed decision. At the same time, policies devised by international peers must be evaluated for their consequences on the policies over extended durations of time.

Several nations have successfully balanced social welfare programmes with fiscal sustainability, leading to stable debt and strong social support systems. On the other hand, some regions facing debt crises and financial instability serve as valuable case examples of the dangers associated with unmanaged debt levels. These case studies can be insightful for many policy practitioners as they develop integrated frameworks to understand the paradoxes and nuances underlying fiscal policies. Additionally, examining the role of global institutions should be part of any comprehensive analysis. Institutions like the International Monetary Fund (IMF) and the World Bank have played a critical role in financially aiding and guiding heavily indebted countries. Understanding these institutions' actions and advice also highlights the importance of international collaboration in multilateral responses to debt problems. With increased globalisation, the significance of cross-border sharing of insights in forming economic policies has never been more critical. Policymakers have more options than ever due to the lessons learned by other nations, enabling them to adopt more suitable and effective policies for national debt reduction and long-term economic stability.

Conclusion: Step Forward in Addressing Economic Policy Issues

The study of various economic policies to address the growing issue of a country's national debt reveals that various countries have different intricacies instituted as international policies. Policies on sustaining long-lasting frameworks are essential during the last stages of dealing with current issues with public debt and fiscal sustainability. It can be noted that some level of debt is manageable as long as sufficient international wisdom is integrated. After finalising what has been explored in this study, some reflections and recommendations that assist in making concrete shifts to sustaining policies are evident.

The first and most important step is encouraging the best practices for achieving fiscal discipline with proper financial operations. Meeting this goal requires long-term thinking, prudent spending, and allocating tangible budgets. Constructing systems that embrace budgetary balance and capping expenditures reduces the 'cutback' mentality and yields a flexible policy environment to enhance long-run growth. Additionally, changing policies that adversely impact revenue collection and introducing new ones that enhance equity and efficiency adds to fairness across different societal groups and ensures greater flexibility within budgetary frameworks.

Recalibrating spending priorities also assumes critical significance in the pursuit of sustainable economic policies. Defining and assessing national priorities and needs in tandem with socio-economic realities allows governments to allocate resources efficiently and invest at the most optimal levels for enduring returns. Moreover, policymakers can plan for sustainable debt management by integrating concise action steps with comprehensive structural reforms and long-term changes to achieve fiscal balance and address the ever-increasing national debt.

The conclusion of this debate emphasises the importance of effective monetary policy not just as a tool for economic stimulus, but about debt control. The careful intertemporal regulation of interest rates, credit availability, and other relevant policy signals by the Federal Reserve's Government guides policy profoundly impacts debt control and economic recovery. At the same time, bipartisan cooperation combined with some other legislative actions above the line reinforces the initiative to design and administer sound economic policies devoid of partisan strife.

In general terms, focusing on and drawing from the successful strategies of other countries fosters collaboration of practices to guide international America and allows peer nations to learn from each other. By studying the gains and setbacks of other countries, the US can develop wise economic policies.

At its core, the journey towards sustainable economic policies requires an integrated approach with a heightened focus on responsible governance and foresight. Addressing the interrelated components of spending control, tax and expenditure realignment, debt alleviation, and international information exchange establishes a robust economic framework to counter the dangers of increasing national debt. As the discussion concludes, the focus must be on implementing these strategies to achieve a sustainable and economically flourishing America for its citizens.

9

Entitlement Programs

Reform Challenges and Opportunities

Overview of the Entitlement Programs

In the American social welfare system context, entitlements form a major pillar, providing economic assistance and healthcare services to eligible beneficiaries. Studying the evolution and intent of such programmes is critical to understanding their effects on the socio-economic dynamics of the country. The roots of entitlements can be found in the New Deal era, which was characterised by President Franklin D. Roosevelt's active efforts to address the problems arising from the Great Depression. During this transformational period, Social Security came into existence – a programme that allowed retired workers to receive income support during their old age. The establishment of Social Security signified a turning point in the Government's role towards its people. It laid the foundation for a sustained commitment to social insurance. Later decades saw the proliferation of entitlement programmes, including Medicare and Medicaid, under President Lyndon B. Johnson's aggressive Great Society policy framework. Medicaid was intended to assist the medical needs of the poor and needy, while elderly citizens received assistance through Medicare. The programmes demonstrated considerable societal acceptance of providing the vulnerable sections of society with aid and assistance.

The American government developed these initiatives to reduce poverty, improve access to healthcare, and promote social welfare. Entitlement programmes expanded and became integrated features of America's social contract based on solidarity, kindness, and help to one another. The socio-economic adversity America faced highlighted why these mechanisms are crucial for protecting millions of citizens. In the coming paragraphs, we will describe each entitlement programme in detail, analysing its financial burdens, sociological issues, and any potential changes needed to maintain optimal efficiency in benefit allocation and fairness while continuing to serve the needs of society.

Historical Evolution and Purpose of Entitlements

As a fundamental part of the American social welfare system, entitlement programmes have developed in response to the needs of the people over time. They can be traced back to the early 20th century with the 1935 Social Security Act, the first federal social insurance programme. This legislation was the first to create a comprehensive system of old-age benefits and shifted the focus to old-age security for citizens. The approach aimed to give relief to those who had worked and contributed their fair share to the economy. With demographic and social changes, the scope and functions of entitlement programmes changed. The Great Society programmes in the 1960s provided Medicare and Medicaid to improve health-care access and affordability for senior and low-income citizens. These programmes were pivotal in expanding social safety nets and demonstrated an obligation towards the provision of fundamental health services. These days, entitlement programmes in all forms strive to minimise the economic crises less privileged groups face and maintain their dignity.

In addition, they have contributed to the development of so-cio-cultural and socio-political stability. The essence of the collective programmes depicts society's socio-spatial responsibility to look after and protect its members, especially the economically or healthily weak. When we explain the background history of entitlements and social policies, we can understand the still-alive marks of compassion, equity, and nurturing in the welfare policies of society. Such comprehension facilitates constructive reflection on the modern problems and prospects of entitlement reform within economics.

Current and Future Interest Impacts of the National Debt

With the ever-increasing magnitude of our national debt, one sharp concern is the fragmentation of society induced by universal healthcare services. Programs guaranteeing certain benefits to specific groups make up significant government expenditure. They are well known to be a major contributing factor to the debt burden, thus raising the dual angle of concern: solvency and sustainability. On top of the already existing socio-economic burden due to the pandemic, the elderly population poses an inevitable challenge in terms of rising healthcare spending. The financial ramifications of such a reality check are calamitous, especially in a world gripped by a pandemic. The perpetual augmentation of universal healthcare programmes is tasked as an incredibly challenging problem because of unsolvable constraints. In the short-sightedness of our policymakers lies the greatest obstacle of all—deferring hope that a maximum amount of national debt could be tolerable to civil society. Addressing the issue by treating the symptoms rather than the cause, holistic reasoning becomes one of the many contemporary buzzwords; rough estimations based on impulsive criticism sprawled in the abstract without context attached to its approach rather than a reasoned policy framework with a keen eye on political feasibility. The flimsy rationalisation used to shred the social contract could only be a product of deeply problematic or, at best, extremely optimistic reasoning. However, it is exceedingly easy to opt for without the need to justify it on any level.

Exploring the intricacies of entitlement spending and its effects on the national debt is vital to stimulating informed debate and enacting constructive policy change. By analysing current fiscal burdens, stakeholders can see how intertwined the entitlement programmes and the national debt are. This analysis serves as a critical foundation needed to construct new, innovative, sustainable, innovative approaches. Understanding how entitlement programmes interact with the fiscal environment calls attention to the pressing need for responsible guardianship of public assets. Moreover, analysing current fiscal impacts relates to balancing short-term goals with long-term objectives, creating sustainable outcomes that maintain budgetary discipline alongside societal commitments. This type of discourse deepens policy responses to the evolving context of entitlement programmes with debt while enhancing contributions to the discussion. This understanding equips leaders, citizens, and scholars with the tools necessary to navigate the intricate web of entitlement reform, ultimately strengthening the nation's finances for the future.

Changing Population Trends: New Challenges to Consider

Due to emerging demographic trends, the structure of entitlement programmes will likely undergo a significant change shortly. Social security and healthcare services will experience a sharp increase in demand because of the ageing baby boomers and increased life expectancy. The changing demographics pose a twofold challenge regarding the funding of these programmes to ensure they are responsive and useful to a population that is changing in many ways. With the growth of the elderly population, there is expected to be a greater deficit in the working population who can support these entitlements, so there is likely to be increased competition in funding these programmes. This captures the problems associated with social security and encompasses healthcare spending because of the increased demand from older individuals who will require more medical and long-term care. Other regions are likely to grapple with these changes, making the fair distribution of resources even more difficult. Accompanied by the problem, there is a need to study population shifts to develop effective policies that address these issues in a timely manner. The focus must be on the range of differences among the different demographic groups, which requires formulating policies that are more responsive and adaptable to changes in the younger entitlement frameworks.

Also, accepting changes in technology in healthcare and eldercare and redefining the concepts of retirement and work are critical aspects of this demographic shift. Developing integrated approaches that consider the holistic consequences of demographic changes is critical in safeguarding the relevance and sustainability of entitlement frameworks. This requires an intricate balance of competing social demands and limited resources to design adaptive and sustainable entitlement systems.

Public perception and political discourse

Public perception and political discourse around entitlement programmes are essential for understanding the issues regarding their reform and long-term sustainability. Their public perception seems to greatly control the political discourse, guiding policies. Whether favourable or unfavourable, public perceptions of entitlements are shaped by personal experience, media, politics, and other external influences. Strong emotions and opinions are often articulated since these programmes directly affect citizens' lives. Therefore, public opinion can mobilise political action either in support of or against the proposed reforms.

The political discourse surrounding entitlement programmes is complex and multidimensional. Disparate party politics, other ideological divides, and electoral politics are responsible for the narrative around entitlements. Politicians and other relevant stakeholders actively seek to advance entitlement programmes as one of the choices in their political agenda. As you will easily glean from political debates over entitlement reform, the contention becomes sharply dichotomised, forcing competing solutions and narratives to be pitched. Such polarisation often contributes to the absence of accurate consensus and dialogue, hindering progress toward meaningful reform.

In addition, important debates on entitlements are increasingly being shaped by biased and unscientific approaches by the media, contributing further to public perception. News articles, alongside opinion editorials, discuss issues on entitlements and contribute to the way they are discussed publicly.

The media's politicisation of entitlement programmes further deepens already-existing divides through biases and sensationalism. On social media, new platforms emerge every day and serve as channels for discussing programmes and welcoming all opinions. However, the same platforms that enable the circulation of a wide range of opinions also enable echo chambers, fostering politically divisive disinformation.

Policymakers seeking to address challenges and reform opportunities must understand public perception and the political discourse surrounding entitlement programmes. The absence of public awareness and a lack of informed discussion create the necessity of fostering a bipartisan dialogue that addresses these complex issues. Striking the balance between opposing viewpoints will shape constructive political discourse and ensure sustainable, equitable provision of entitlement programmes for future generations.

Comparative Analysis: Global Models of Welfare Entitlements

The diversity of social, political and economic structures in different countries is why programmes such as government subsidies and support services, especially social security and healthcare systems, are shaped differently worldwide. A study contrasting the various frameworks of these programmes shows the social welfare systems of healthcare and social security services in one country relative to another can unveil the pros, cons, and other unexploited possibilities of improvement in the welfare service. Many European countries were pioneers in building comprehensive welfare states characterised by advanced social security and public healthcare systems. These programmes provide a safety net for citizens; however, sustainability-related challenges due to ageing populations and rising healthcare costs are a problem. Some Asian countries, in contrast, have more focused and means-tested entitlement programmes that emphasise poverty alleviation and incentivise workforce participation, addressing social and economic issues. These systems are effective but lack the universality necessary to address income inequality. In Australia and New Zealand, social investment has become dominant, focusing on proactive and tailored support, early implementation of interventions, and evaluation of programme outcomes to optimise long-term benefits. Canada has implemented a mixed model, combining universal healthcare with social assistance, demonstrating public healthcare policy and fiscal prudence. A review of these international examples raises questions about the construction, implementation, and efficiency of social support programmes offered in the United

States.

Studying global best practices is crucial for policymakers, advocates, and the general public. It provides a comprehensive understanding of the issues and potential reforms needed to maintain sustainability, equity, and efficiency within the entitlement framework.

Innovative Principles and Legislative Solutions

Policymakers are challenged with developing comprehensive strategy plans and proposals to ensure longevity as programmes classified under entitlements undergo constant alterations due to societal factors and economic pressures. Specific strategies have been developed to address the fiscal and demographic difficulties confronting programmes classified under entitlement. One such proposal is means-tested benefits, which seeks to reduce entitlement payments to individuals of higher income, allowing payment resources to those who truly require assistance. Another important idea that is being implemented is shifting the retirement age and entitlement age to allow for a greater number of years lived and worked. These reforms aim to help ease the strain upon entitlement programmes due to the ageing population and shifting workforce trends.

When these solutions are fashioned bipartisan, utilising cross-party and cross-ideology coalitions, they can be assembled into a much stronger and more cohesive policy, ensuring that all voices are heard and valued in the process.

As with the management and supervision of entitlement programmes, promoting transparency and responsibility is still important. Better control of administrative burden and data processes, along with technology and analytics, improves efficiency and reduces fraud and improper payments. Evidence-based policy design places power in decision-makers' hands by using applicable research, evidence, and best practices for self-assessment, evaluation, and reform initiatives. Also, some targeted cost containment strategies like negotiation, utilisation management, and care coordination can lead to significant savings without lowering the quality of care or benefits provided. Broader education and targeted outreach are necessary to ensure complete comprehension and support from the public regarding the proposed reforms by highlighting the impact on fiscal sustainability and fair distribution of social safety nets. Explaining the need for change without myths is surely helpful in gaining public confidence. In general, balanced reform ideas and carefully drafted legislative proposals form the foundation to enhance the responsiveness and flexibility of entitlement programmes to changes in socio-economic conditions.

Balancing Act: Innovation vs. Tradition

When analysing the ongoing debate about entitlement programmes, one notable imbalance is the failure to focus on the need to innovate to address societal challenges while also respecting the traditional frameworks embedded within these programmes. Social systems have a strong tendency to change dynamically, and the need for innovation is acute. However, one has to also think about the core values that support these principles with regard to social entitlement programmes.

Innovation within entitlement programmes includes a wide range of activities, such as modernising the administrative functions of the programme, technological upgrades, and enhancing service delivery and accessibility to beneficiaries. The application of data and artificial intelligence can certainly be useful in increasing the programme's efficiency, making appropriate resource distributions, and minimising fraud and abuse. In addition, implementing new ideas can improve the functioning of bureaucratic processes and other institutional frameworks, enabling the responsiveness of these programmes to contemporary needs.

On the other hand, preserving tradition underlines the maintenance of societal obligations and the protection of fundamental rights and benefits that entitlement programmes provide. It demands respect for the history of these programmes while not deviating from their primary intended use. Uplifting traditions brings about stability, which helps anchor entitlement programmes into the values of social cohesion, charity, fairness, and compassion. It helps pay respect to the contributions and sacrifices of different generations, which strengthens the civic commitment of inter-generational responsibility and reciprocity.

The relationship between innovation and tradition is equally puzzling, with all the underlying issues that must be thoughtfully steered towards achieving a balance in co-existence. Striking harmony is about meeting progress requirements while ensuring foundational values are not altered. This considers the ethical and moral frameworks of forward-thinking propositions and their integration into entitlement programmes without stripping away the core foundations. Achieving this balance also requires considering the varying perspectives of other beneficiaries while ensuring disruptive change is kept to a minimum during transformative approaches.

In addition, resolving the conflict of innovation versus tradition requires the participation of stakeholders in constructive dialogues and, more importantly, in collaboration. Policymakers,

advocates, beneficiaries, and the entire community must think together about balancing the potential offered by modern approaches and the importance of traditional methods. Through respectful
discourse to build understanding around differing perspectives,
it is possible to formulate an agreement that seeks progress while
retaining essential features of entitlement programmes.

As noted, the interplay of innovation and tradition within entitlement programmes seeks a dynamic balance. Seeking change
while also preserving fundamental features of public services will
ensure responsiveness to global programming trends. Innovation
regarding services offered should be counterbalanced with emphasis on the obligation to provide such services, thereby safeguarding
effective response systems.

Stakeholder Interests and Collaborative Solutions

The spectrum of stakeholder interests in entitlement programmes
captures government agencies, policymakers, advocacy groups,
employers, employees, and the general public. Each stakeholder has a unique outlook and set of priorities regarding the design, maintenance, and reform of entitlement programmes. Government agencies must ensure benefit delivery, cost control, and
programme integrity. Policymakers attempt to respond to constituents' needs while considering social spending and other concerns. Advocacy groups represent some beneficiary populations
and work out policies for them to ensure safe and equitable access
to these programmes. Employers and employees are concerned
with the financial viability and enduring nature of such programmes because there is a payroll tax and economic competition
for jobs in the region. The general public's concern for these pro-

grammes stems from the need for a safety net that offers economic assurance and reliability.

Collaborative approaches are critical for addressing these stakeholders' particular issues and interests. Multistakeholder dialogues, forums, and advisory boards serve as opportunities for constructive dialogues and reaching a common agreement. These constructive engagements allow stakeholders to share insights and best practices and create integrated action plans from various approaches. In addition, collaboration can stimulate innovation in the design and administration of programmes, thus enabling more precise targeting of aid to the intended beneficiaries. Applying different stakeholders' skills and resources makes it possible to design sustainable, evidence-based reforms that can weather politically tumultuous environments and sustain bipartisan support. Collaboration in reforming entitlement programmes can give stakeholders a sense of shared ownership and responsibility, encouraging broader public support while strengthening trust in social welfare programmes.

Collaboration considers intergenerational equity together with long-term economic sustainability while developing solutions. Paying attention to demographic changes and their effects on entitlement programme finances is important to address. Sustained open conversations and collaborations across generational divides can help design policies that attend to the needs of current beneficiaries and those anticipated in future decades. It is necessary to consider the trade-off between providing immediate relief and exercising long-term fiscal restraint, emphasising the need to provide enduring solutions that protect programme support, viability, and availability to future generations. Equitable and sufficient solutions need to be crafted before fractures so that political partisanship is irrelevant while ensuring entitlement programmes are kept alive purposefully within society's ever-changing socio-economic environment. Programmes remain functional as intended without straying from the core purpose in focus while addressing responsiveness and elasticity.

Future Directions and Long-Term Sustainability

As highlighted above, sustainability entails managing the long-term effectiveness of these programmes well ahead of time. The work requires outpacing superficial political interests devoid of critical thought. Evidence-based decision-making, anticipatory governance, and sharp spending control all contribute to a shifting mindset towards recalibrating entitlement programmes that serve all current and prospective generations.

10

Learning from History

Can America Avoid a Debt Catastrophe?

Analysing Historical Debt Crises: Lessons Learned

Excessive debt burdens have been problematic for various countries throughout history. Understanding the root causes of these historical debt crises provides us with critical insights into their primary causes, which could enable us to adopt measures to circumvent similar situations in the future. A review of past debt crises reveals patterns of unregulated expenditure by governments, over-borrowing, economic recessions, and, consequently, a shrinking revenue base. The 1980s Latin American debt crisis is a classic example of unscrupulous dependence on foreign loans with high-risk exchange rates, and the 2008 global debt crisis high-lighted the interdependence of complicated financial instruments and debt-fuelled depression. Historical debt crises also illuminated the severe impact of a lack of supervision and poor economic governance, erratic fiscal policies, and an underappreciation of the risks posed by systemic financial frailties. It also draws attention to the absence of active policies to counter systemic financial vulnerabilities. Emphasis on restructuring debt crises underscores the importance of progressive guiding policy on unambiguously reforming debt and governance restructuring under accountability. These observations demonstrate that countries that focused on fiscal discipline developed sound regulatory policies, and promoted economic growth were the ones that overcame these debt disasters.

These particular case studies underscore the crucial role of proactive risk management, responsible fiscal policies, and the imperative of fostering long-term economic growth. A comprehensive understanding of debt crises throughout history empowers stakeholders and policymakers to devise robust plans to effectively manage escalating national debt and transition towards sustainable fiscal policies, instilling a sense of confidence in the potential for preventing future debt crises.

Comparative Case Studies: Successful Interventions

Comparative case studies are especially important in the analysis of debt management. When studying cases in which countries had sizable debt burdens, fundamental insights can be gleaned from the successful interventions these nations undertook. This insight can help mitigate modern-day approaches to debt risk. These empirical case studies provide evidence of successful and unsuccessful attempts at combating debt crises. One of the most prominent case studies is Canada's economic turnaround in the 1990s. The Canadian Government's debt levels were severely high, and the economy was stagnant. The Canadian Government implemented many bold strategies, including aggressive spending cuts and structural reforms. Not only did this succinct action restore fiscal balance, but it also increased investor confidence, providing a platform for improved economic growth. Other countries, such as Sweden and New Zealand, have also faced severe debt challenges, which they confronted head-on, proving to be immensely disciplined with their finances. After analysing these case studies, economists and policymakers can devise effective patterns and principles for debt intervention strategies.

By analysing the specific programmes and actions that were successful within different countries, it is possible to identify relevant practices that do not change regardless of geographical or temporal borders. These case studies highlight the importance of political will, civic action, and multifactor stakeholder change coalitions. They illustrate the need for cooperation and collective agreement across party lines to develop policies preventing a debt catastrophe spiral for the nation. Learning from the experiences of other countries, such as the UK's successful debt reduction strategy in the 19th century or Germany's post-war economic recovery, enhances understanding of the debt management phenomena and equips them to make informed decisions. Through rigorous analysis of comparative case studies, this chapter aims to unlock better historical successes—proactive, pragmatic strategies for debt alleviation will be guided by them.

The Contribution of Fiscal Policy Towards Preventing Debt

The undeniable truth is that the fiscal policy of any nation significantly shapes its economic pathway, and consequently, influences how a nation manages its debt. A prudent and effective fiscal policy means that appropriate public spending, taxation, and borrowing policies are in place. These aspects, in turn, govern any economy's debt level. By maintaining proper fiscal policies, a government can steer clear of excessive debt burdens that may lead to financial crises in the future, providing the audience with a clear understanding of the impact of fiscal decisions on the economy.

Debt prevention relies largely on managing public expenditure, which is part of fiscal policy. Expenditure in public budgeting is directed towards activities or areas funded that can stimulate socio-economic growth. Proper public spending means that resources are used towards enhancing growth and societal benefits without engaging in unnecessary spending that heavily drains the national budget. Solid budgeting alongside rigorous scrutiny of expenditure reduces the likelihood of accumulating debt.

Equally important is the strategic design of the taxation system in relation to fiscal policy. A properly formulated tax policy offers revenue for state activities, serves income redistribution, and stabilises the economy. Provided with an adequate taxation system that fosters compliance and null evasion, a government can improve its fiscal position and decrease its dependence on public services and goods debt financing. Also, particular taxation that encourages investment and economic activity can improve revenue and ease the strain on public finances.

Debt prevention incorporates prudent borrowing in fiscal policy. Well-responsible borrowing governments tend to be more prudent in resorting to external financing because of the implications of accumulating debt. They monitor the dynamics of the debt along with debt reduction and capital expenditure limits to control the cost of borrowing and ensure the funds borrowed will grow with sustainable investments. To maintain investors, strong market credibility and credit pointing are required from the government, and there needs to be clarity in defining responsibility and accountability in the decision concerning the debt.

Moreover, the establishment of definitive borderlines and institutional frameworks can serve as a preventive measure to avert debt incurrence. Strategic fiscal protocols like instituting debt limits and balanced budgets require legislation that makes it compulsory to control government debt and expenditure, thereby preventing the generation of excess debt. Similarly, the creation of independent governing bodies, such as autonomous fiscal watchdogs, whose responsibilities include overseeing budgetary self-restraint and issuing reliable forecasts, can enhance markets' trust and eliminate irresponsible fiscal behaviour, ensuring the stability of the financial system.

In conclusion, the responsibility of fiscal policy in stopping spending is far more intricate and sophisticated because it requires reevaluating focus areas that emphasise economic activity, social outcome and enduring equilibrium simultaneously. With careful monitoring, countries can identify spending, taxes, and loans on the right side of the policy spectrum. As a result, it becomes possible to avert self-inflicted harms and simultaneously regulatory collapses whilst maintaining bearing frameworks of responsibility.

Managing Debt: Efficient Practices

Sustained economic growth and public finances of a nation with manageable public debt levels require effective debt management. Best practices in debt management are multi-faceted and systematic. One such practice is to set and achieve specific fiscal objectives. This activity includes setting appropriate debt targets that must be met and maintained without surpassing the balance between public expenditure and income. It also means that adequate finance is available to meet public obligations. These practices should be elementary and focus on the governance framework, which increases and manages debt in an accountable manner to reduce the risks associated with debt accumulation. There is a need for a comprehensive strategy concerning the governance framework of debt management, with the appropriate assessment of risks, optimised costs, and solid monitoring structures. There is justification that governments improve their position concerning exposure to currency and interest rate risks by widening the base of debt holders and issuing debts in other currencies. Moreover, the creation of an active and developed market for domestic bonds helps in the restructuring of repayment schedules of outstanding obligations. It reduces the risks associated with rolling over obligations set in bonds. A more effective debt management system is achieved if a country works with other financial institutions and uses its capacity to strengthen debt management.

As with all markets, adapting to the rapidly changing conditions involves reevaluating the approaches taken with debt management and leveraging new financial tools and technologies. Constructive approaches towards managing or mitigating debt with the necessary stakeholders, including the investors, instil confidence that the government takes the issue of fiscal responsibility seriously. Additionally, nurturing responsible public debt by fostering awareness of debt and cultivating financial literacy among citizens creates a more informed society. Implementing these practices enables governments to manage debt efficiently while protecting economies from potential crises and ensuring long-term economic stability.

Preventative Strategy of Economic Diversification

Economic diversification is known to be a key preventative step to take to reduce the impact of debt distress. Economies that depend heavily on one sector tend to be quite vulnerable to market downturns. When a country supports and embraces economic diversification, it can enhance its resilience by distributing risks across different sectors. From the perspective of debt prevention, this strategy carries several benefits. First, economically diversified countries are buffered from external shocks such as global recessions or interruptions in particular industry fuels. Second, a diverse economy stimulates entrepreneurial undertakings and innovations which sustain long-term growth. Increased economic activity will likely raise tax collection and lower expenditures on public services due to reduced borrowing. Furthermore, economic diversification assists in the dissemination of new job opportunities and the attraction of skilled labour, which will reduce the increase in unemployment levels and elevate the overall standard of living. Many countries have successfully implemented economic diversification, such as Singapore, Norway, and the United Arab Emirates, which have all reaped the benefits of carefully directed investments and diversification.

The sustainable economic development incorporating advanced technology and fostering entrepreneurship with low incurred debt underwent optimal utilisation of resources. These shifts aimed at tackling the problem of having a vision and implementing policies to diversify the economy motivated leadership. Government intervention was necessary to pioneer various industries by providing initial funding, necessary infrastructure, and specific vocational training to relevant disciplines. Through these alliances, the educational sector can also foster innovative changes to accelerate diversification policies. In addition, encouraging active citizen participation highlights the idea of economic diversification and guarantees an economy that benefits all members of this society. This policy represents one of the core strategies devised to strengthen the financial position and overall economic stability, ensuring a preventative measure against the anticipated debt disaster and navigating towards sustained growth.

Public Awareness and Political Responsibility

Public awareness and political responsibility play a pivotal role in addressing the national debt problem. A comprehensive approach, which involves multiple aspects, is essential. It's not just about economic or technological solutions. Public awareness, starting with educating citizens about the consequences of growing national debt, is crucial. This includes understanding how excessive debt stifles economic growth, increases interest rates, and burdens future generations. With adequate education, the public can learn the complexities surrounding fiscal policies and make rational decisions while voting for their economic policy. Also, in combination with the factors above, the attenuation of responsible spending at the grassroots level can enhance the outlook for the economy.

Political responsibility is a key factor in averting a debt crisis. It's just as important as public awareness. Political leaders need to safeguard the nation's fiscal sustainability in the long run over any short-term gains by exercising proper control over budgets and spending. A politically responsible government should be accountable for curbing the deficit by practising transparency in government spending. In addition, the politically responsible government must work together across party lines to deal with the complexity of fiscal policy.

Rather than focusing on partisan politics, it is more favourable for policymakers to work on rational fiscal reforms which will help achieve extensive and long-term economic growth. In addition, political leaders need to talk clearly with constituents to explain the need for fiscal restraint while garnering support and public opinion for the tough measures that must be taken. When political leaders trust their constituents and talk to them openly while making decisions publicly, the people tend to take collective ownership of the country's finances rather than becoming passive observers. All in all, from caring deeply about the national debt solution to being politically responsible, both concepts are needed in a nurturing environment if meaningful change is ever to arise concerning national debt issues.

Innovative Technology: Reducing Financial Strain

Innovative technology can be extremely beneficial, especially for those feeling the pressure of national debts and economic instability, since it works toward resolving financial issues and enabling greater responsibility. The advancement of technology specifically aims to streamline processes, help create new optimisations for resource allocation, and improve how finances are managed, especially in the public sector. When focusing on public finance, there are many opportunities due to technological innovation that can significantly improve debt reduction and achieve sustainable economic growth.

The application of advanced analytic techniques, particularly through AI systems, marks one of the most impactful opportunities for technological innovation aimed at cost efficiency. With the availability of big data and advanced algorithmic AI, governments can now understand spending, revenue, and debt flow like never before. This new understanding allows for much more informed decisions to be made in the distribution of resources. Furthermore, AI can help develop future economic trend projections and identify potential risks, allowing policymakers to mitigate emerging problems and avert debt crises.

The other major area of focus regarding integrating new technologies is upgrading the financial system and payment methods to include digital and cashless systems. Moving to cashless payments and digital currency helps governments improve efficiency, reduce financial crime, and lower costs. These payment methods also encourage real-time monitoring of expenditures, improving accountability and curtailing the misuse of funds. On the other hand, blockchain technology facilitates reliable and transparent record-keeping that improves fiscal discipline and reduces the chances of fraud.

Innovative technology enhances financial management and aids in optimising revenue collection and tax administration. Sophisticated digital solutions can simplify compliance with tax obligations, lower administrative costs, curb non-compliance through improved data checks, and strengthen identification measures. Modern technology ensures equal taxation by providing real-time reporting and automated auditing, which allows governments to expand their revenue streams and lessen the burden of regulations on citizens.

Moreover, the application of FinTech allows for easier access to credit and investment for small and medium enterprises (SMEs). Through advanced digital lending and investment tools, governments can promote self-employment and economic growth and, as a result, reduce the burden of public debt. Furthermore, projects promoting financial services for the underprivileged enable active socio-economic integration and decrease reliance on government aid.

To sum up, it is clear that the most innovative technological developments lower expenses and increase cost efficiency. The adoption of new technology in public finance increases the ease of management operations and advances stronger discipline, accountability, and sustainable economic management. While struggling with persistent structural fiscal obstacles, integrating technology into debt management helps countries prepare for the best possible fiscal future.

As countries become increasingly dependent on each other, the need for international collaborations to tackle economic volatility and promote sustainable growth becomes more pronounced. This interconnectedness underscores the importance of collective action and cooperation in fostering economic stability globally, making the audience feel a sense of shared responsibility in the face of economic challenges.

The International Monetary Fund and World Bank initiatives are crucial focal points for fostering global collaborations. These institutions stabilise the volatile economies of member countries by offering financial aid, technical support, and policy guidance. Moreover, regular consultations among principal economies and emerging markets foster bilateral understanding and cooperation in reacting to economic disturbances.

Agreements and alliances significantly enhance a country's economic stability. Such agreements allow for new market opportunities, help them expand their export options, and build a strong economy. Moreover, joint regulatory mechanisms and supervisory frameworks can reduce the threats that come with global financial interrelationships, making them more stable.

Regarding monetary policies, exchange rate fluctuations, capital flows, charge differentials, and interest rates usually require the attention of central banks working in collaboration. Countries can stabilise currency trading's speculative attempts while fighting currency depreciation, thereby improving the overall economy.

A multi-dimensional approach is required to achieve sustainable development goals. The commitments allied towards environmental protection, lifting people out of poverty, and building essential structures needed globally are unarguably the most important economic collaborations that are needed. These factors reinforce economic resilience while assisting in reaching these unprecedented goals internationally.

A synergistic approach on an international level to dealing with systemic risks like pandemics, cyber threats, natural hazards, and any other disaster is a necessity. Such preemptive measures are crucial to increasing economic stability through collaborative risk assessment, strategised contingency planning, and crisis management.

In the end, the goal of global cooperation to maintain economic equilibrium requires an integrated framework surpassing geopolitical or ideological boundaries. Working collaboratively makes it easier to navigate the modern complex global economy by creating an everlasting foundation for stability if individual countries focus on achieving collective success rather than seeking personal benefits.

Future Scenarios: Predictive Models and Analysis

Anticipating and managing potential future debt crises is one of the key challenges to address in the global economy.

Through predictive models and thorough analysis, experts and policymakers can carve out efficient paths to defend against possible financial calamities by gaining foresight about different situations through proactive actions while exploring potential policy frameworks. By reviewing historical data and using sophisticated econometric approaches, economists can accurately capture diverse economic variables alongside external factors in dynamic econometric systems, which simulate different scenarios through stepwise changing processes and highlight critical economic structural voids and tipping points.

Furthermore, early warning systems enable governments and fiscal institutions to detect potential debt crises using predictive analysis through emerging trends and patterns. By enabling proactive, carefully planned policy modifications, financial institutions and governments can reduce the risk of a downturn. Predictive modelling through advanced data analytics and artificial intelligence can estimate the rate of debt increase, interest, and fiscal deficits, making it easier to draft rational policies that protect the economy long-term.

Other than these benefits, predictive analysis can be paired with scenario planning and stress testing for more holistic assessments of future models. Geopolitical uncertainties, unplanned external shocks, and unpredictable market behaviours may create significant obstacles to accurate forecasting.

Nations worldwide can collaborate by sharing and collecting information to improve the reliability of predictive models internationally. Collaborative research and information exchange between nations promotes the understanding of global economics. Advanced predictive ability allows countries to protect the international financial system from risks and debt-related disruptions through cooperative modelling.

To wrap up, the most effective way to tackle the multifaceted challenges presented by possible future debt situations is to apply advanced predictive modelling techniques and systematic analyses. Utilising data analytics and collective planning, leaders can effectively manage an economy to guide it towards a safe and sustainable path that remains intact through possible debt crises.

Conclusion: Developing a Strategy for Debt Problem Resolution

Considering the increasingly complicated problem of debt mitigation, it is clear that a blend of diverse sparring strategies is the most effective in solving such an intricate problem. With the help of predictive models coupled with robust historical analysis, we have gained insights into the foretelling future debt scenario. Predictions are insufficient; something more proactive is needed, such as holistic fiscal policies aimed at controlling debt through restructuring policies along with the management that comes with them. A keen focus on a few critical components is essential to build such measures. To begin with, the economic vulnerabilities that stem from a lack of diversification vis-à-vis excessive government debts, especially for developing nations should be effectively safeguarded. It is necessary to deal with excessive borrowing, which is made possible by diversified economic systems. In addition to these, a heightened sense of public responsibility aids in reducing debt, a political obligation that needs to be taught throughout the country. Thus, growing awareness of the national debt requires action beyond civil discourse, and policymakers must act responsibly. Additionally, governments must implement sound expenditure policies instead of relying on politics within the parties. Concerning financial burdens, the importance of innovative technological measures cannot be overstated.

Adopting modern financial technologies can simplify budgetary activities, improve transparency, and reduce wasteful spending, thus helping to reduce debt. Additionally, promoting global partnerships for economic stability is still crucial within the global context. International cooperation through dialogues, strategic partnerships, and coordinated actions with other countries can strengthen the capacity to withstand economic shocks and effectively manage sustainable debt levels. However, no approach towards mitigating debt can be effective without full measures for crisis prevention. Successful strategies from comparative case studies suggest that necessary pre-emptive actions must be taken to avert the economy's deep-seated vulnerabilities from becoming crises. This systematic and proactive perspective allows for an effective approach towards debt mitigation. To sum up, addressing the intricate challenges of national debt requires an integrated and multi-faceted combination of strategies focused on responsible spending, technology, international collaboration, and active crisis prevention. Draw these principles into a singular strategy, and countries can set themselves on a proven sustainable path towards solving debt issues and securing a strong economic future.

Selected Bibliograpy

On the rise of US debt in history, from colonial America to pre-Reagan fiscal policies

- Bordo, M. D., & White, E. N. (1991). A tale of two currencies: British and French finance during the Napoleonic Wars. *The Journal of Economic History, 51*(2), 303–316.

- Brownlee, W. E. (2004). *Federal taxation in America: A short history* (2nd ed.). Cambridge University Press.

- Ferguson, N. (2001). *The cash nexus: Money and power in the modern world, 1700–2000.* Basic Books.

- Friedman, M., & Schwartz, A. J. (1971). *A monetary history of the United States, 1867–1960.* Princeton University Press.

- Goldsmith, R. W. (1969). *Financial structure and devel-*

opment. Yale University Press.

- Gordon, J. (1998). *Hamilton's blessing: The extraordinary life and times of our national debt.* Penguin Books.

- Hall, S. W. (1943). War borrowing practices in early America. *The American Economic Review, 33*(2), 258–266.

- Hammond, B. (1957). *Banks and politics in America, from the Revolution to the Civil War.* Princeton University Press.

- McDonald, F. (1985). *The presidency of Thomas Jefferson: The origins of America's fiscal policies.* Oxford University Press.

- North, D. C., & Weingast, B. R. (1989). Constitutions and commitment: The evolution of institutions governing public choice in seventeenth-century England. *The Journal of Economic History, 49*(4), 803–832. (Contextual analysis linked to colonial influence on fiscal policies.)

- Rauchway, E. (2008). *The Great Depression and the New Deal: A very short introduction.* Oxford University Press.

- Rockoff, H. (1984). Price and wage controls in four wartime periods. *The Journal of Economic History, 44*(1), 76–84.

- Scheiber, H. N. (1975). *The state and the economy: Interrelations in American history.* Academic Press.

- Sutch, R., & Carter, S. B. (2006). *Historical statistics of the United States: Earliest times to the present.* Cambridge University Press.

- Wicker, E. (1960). Colonial monetary standards contrasted: Evidence from individual balance sheets. *The Journal of Economic History, 20*(3), 419–436.

These entries span the founding of the US, early financial policies, debt association with war, fiscal developments during industrialization, and pre-Reagan debt formation. Several might be nonlinear but provide depth to build a historical understanding of US debt trends.

More on the Debt in History

America's Debt Burden. (1940). *Bankers' Magazine (1896-1943), 140*(6), 498.

AMERICA'S DEBT TO AFRICA. (1885). *The African Repository (1850-1892), 61*(4), 109.

AMERICA'S DEBT TO ENGLAND: CONCLUSION OF ADDRESS BY CANON FARRAR AT CHICKERING HALL, N. Y., TENTH MONTH 29TH, 1886. (1889, Jul 25). *Friends' Review; a Religious, Literary and Miscellaneous Journal (1847-1894), 42*, 828.

America's Debt to Israel. (1905, Dec 09). *Outlook (1893-1924), 81*, 857.

AMERICA'S DEBT TO KOSCIUSKO: HERO OF TWO CONTINENTS ARRIVED HERE 150 YEARS AGO. (1926, Jul 17). *The Independent (1922-1928), 117*, 62.

AMERICA'S DEBT TO THE GERMANS. (1911, Aug 03).

The Youth's Companion (1827-1929), 85, 392.

AMERICA'S DEBT TO THE INDIANS. (1904, Jun 30). *New York Observer and Chronicle (1833-1912), 82*, 823.

AMERICA'S EDUCATIONAL DEBT TO PRUSSIA: AN ACCOUNT OF IMPORTANT REFORMS IN OUR PUB-LIC-SCHOOL SYSTEM THAT WERE "MADE IN GER-MANV". (1918, 12). *Current Opinion (1913-1925), OL. LXV*, 386.

BOOKS RECEIVED. (1871). *The Journal of Speculative Philosophy (1867-1893), 5*(4), 375.

EXPANSION OF CREDIT IN THE UNITED STATES.: GROWTH OF OUR FOREIGN TRADE. EUROPEAN OPINION REGARDING AMERICAN BUSINESS DEVEL-OPMENT. INDICATIONS OF A TURN OF THE TIDE. THE RISE IN BANK CREDITS AND DECLINE IN BANK RESERVES. THE INCREASE OF FIXED INVESTMENTS. ADVANCE IN THE PRICES OF COMMODITIES. AMERI-CA'S FLOATING DEBT TO EUROPE. (1902). *Bankers' Magazine (1896-1943), 65*(5), 611.

Great Britain Asks Debt Payment: Note to France and Other Allies Says Payment is Made Necessary by Attitude of United States SEEKS ONLY TO PAY DEBT. (1922). *Bankers' Magazine (1896-1943), 105*(3), 449.

International Banking and Finance: War Loans REVO-LUTIONARY LOANS FIRST DOMESTIC LOAN FIRST BANK OF ISSUE HAMILTON'S FUNDING POLICY WAR OF 1812 MEXICAN WAR LOANS CIVIL WAR LOANS DEFICIT IN 1863 A POPULAR LOAN PRE-SERVED AMERICA'S IDEALS FOREIGN WAR LOANS INCREASE IN FINANCIAL STRENGTH BASIS FOR FOREIGN LOANS LOANS MEAN INSURANCE FIXED

INCOME FROM INTEREST COMMERCE DEPENDS ON CREDIT "INEXHAUSTIBLE RESOURCES" BRITISH CHANCELLOR'S ASSERTION BRITISH-FRENCH IN-COME BRITISH-FRENCH WEALTH WAR DEBT AND IN-COME AN ASTONISHING PARALLEL DEBT AND SE-CURITY PRICES EARLIER WAR OUTLAYS ENTERPRISE UNCHECKED IMPROOVED ECONOMIC RELATIONS AMERICA'S OPPORTUNITY EXTERNAL LOANS SAFE. (1917). *Bankers' Magazine (1896-1943)*, *94*(4), 402.

The Philippine Tariff Bill: The Republican and Democratic Reports Other Work of Congress The Cuban Sugar Question The Crisis in Cuba The Schley Case Public Opinion Civil Service Reform The Pennsylvania's Tunnel The Pennsylvania's Station The Southern Securities Company America's Debt Abroad Telephone Extension Through Message Rates Germany and the Poles The Boer Concentration Camps Missionaries in South China Missionaries in North China Roman Catholic Federation Mr. Abbey's "Holy Grail" Transatlantic Wireless Telegraphy. (1901, Dec 21). *Outlook (1893-1924)*, *69*, 1001.

War Debt Cancellation Urged: CANCELLATION OF THE ALLIED DEBT WOULD BE THE GREATEST POSSIBLE PANACEA. (1921). *Bankers' Magazine (1896-1943)*, *102*(6), 997.

Bigelow, P. (1900, Jul 05). America's Debt to Germany. *The Independent...Devoted to the Consideration of Politics, Social and Economic Tendencies, History, Literature, and the Arts (1848-1921)*, *52*, 1605.

Lamont, T. W. (1927). AMERICA'S FOREIGN INVESTMENT POLICY: THE MEXICAN DEBT SITUATION THE SITUATION OF NICARAGUA AMERICA'S AID TO HAITI THE RECORD OF SAN DOMINGO THE CHANGE

IN AMERICA'S CREDIT POSITION WHERE AMERICAN LOANS HAVE GONE ESTIMATED VALUE OF AMERI-CAN INVESTMENTS ABROAD ON DECEMBER 31, 1925 (IN MILLIONS) LOANS TO CENTRAL EUROPE FOR-EIGN GOVERNMENT, STATE, MUNICIPAL AND COR-PORATE LOANS PUBLICLY ISSUED IN THE UNITED STATES FROM 1919 (THE ARMISTICE) TO 1926 INCLU-SIVE LOANS TO JAPAN AND AUSTRALIA ARGENTINE LOANS THE POSITION OF FRANCE AND ITALY WILL AMERICA CONTINUE TO LEND ON SAME SCALE? CAN AMERICA MEET DAWES PLAN PAYMENTS? EU-ROPE BECOMING MORE UNIFIED LOOKING FOR-WARD TO A CHANGED EUROPE. *Bankers' Magazine (1896-1943), 114*(6), 871.

M, W. S. (1896, Nov 26). America's Debt and Duty. *The Independent ...Devoted to the Consideration of Politics, Social and Economic Tendencies, History, Literature, and the Arts (1848-1921), 48*, 1.

Peek, W. J. (1908, Aug 27). AMERICA'S DEBT TO THE INDIAN.: "BERTHOLD MISSION CONQUERING THE RED MAN FOR CHRIST.". *New York Observer and Chronicle (1833-1912), 86*, 274.

Pettee, J. H. (1887, 04). AMERICA'S DEBT TO JAPAN! *The Missionary Herald, Containing the Proceedings of the American Board of Commissioners for Foreign Missions (1821-1906), 83*, 136.

Robinson, H. M. (1925). American Banking and World Rehabilitation: Should Conditions Be Imposed as to Use of Proceeds of Loans to Foreign Borrowers? U. S. is Only Nation to Show Advance Over 1913 in World Trade United States in Position of Commercial Banker The Present Situation Abroad The Balance

Sheet for 1924 Debts Can Be paid in Only Two Ways Getting Value of Allies' Credits out of Germany America's Part in Projects Financed A Typical Project A Suggested Clearing House of Information. *Bankers' Magazine (1896-1943), 111*(2), 205.

Other Sources and References

Abdo Elnakouri, Huynh, A. C., & Grossmann, I. (2024). Explaining contentious political issues promotes open-minded thinking. *Cognition*, *247*, 105769. https://doi.org/10.1016/j.cognition.2024.105769

Abdou, H. A., Elamer, A. A., Abedin, M. Z., & Ibrahim, B. A. (2024). The impact of oil and global markets on Saudi stock market predictability: A machine learning approach. *Energy Economics*, *132*, 107416. https://doi.org/10.1016/j.eneco.2024.107416

Ahmed, H. A., Mahmood, S., & Hedieh Shadmani. (2022). Defense and Non-defense vs Debt: How does defense and non-defense government spending impact the dynamics of federal government debt in the United States? *Journal of Government and Economics*, *7*, 100050. https://doi.org/10.1016/j.jge.2022.100050

Aizenman, J., Beirne, J., Chinn, M. D., Yothin Jinjarak, & Park, D. (2024). Monetary and fiscal policy challenges in emerging markets amid elevated uncertainty. *Journal of International Money and Finance*, *149*, 103199. https://doi.org/10.1016/j.jimonfin.2024.103199

Akiba, C. F., Smith, J., Wenger, L. D., Morris, T., Patel, S. V., Bluthenthal, R. N., Tookes, H. E., LaKosky, P., Kral, A. H., & Lambdin, B. H. (2024). Financial barriers, facilitators, and strategies among syringe services programs in the U.S., and their impact on implementation and health outcomes. *SSM - Qualitative Re-*

search in Health, *5*, 100421. https://doi.org/10.1016/j.ssmqr.20 24.100421

Akira Kamiguchi, & Tamai, T. (2023). Public investment, national debt, and economic growth: The role of debt finance under dynamic inefficiency. *Journal of Macroeconomics*, *77*, 103535. ht tps://doi.org/10.1016/j.jmacro.2023.103535

Ali, S., Naveed, M., Al-Nassar, N. S., & Mirza, N. (2024). Mineral Metamorphosis: Tracing the static and dynamic nexus between minerals and global south markets. *Resources Policy*, *96*, 105222. https://doi.org/10.1016/j.resourpol.2024.105222

Alva, A., Dunning, K., Williamson, R., & Kampol Pannoi. (2024). What compels bipartisan lawmakers to support coral reef legislation in the U.S. Congress. *Marine Policy*, *163*, 106094. htt ps://doi.org/10.1016/j.marpol.2024.106094

Amin Mohseni-Cheraghlou. (2016). The aftermath of financial crises: A look on human and social wellbeing. *World Development*, *87*, 88–106. https://doi.org/10.1016/j.worlddev.2016.06.001

Andolfatto, D., & Gervais, M. (2008). Endogenous debt constraints in a life-cycle model with an application to social security. *Journal of Economic Dynamics and Control*, *32*, 12. https://doi.o rg/10.1016/j.jedc.2008.03.005

Andrés, C., & Chamorro, A. (2025). Fiscal asymmetries under a debt consolidation strategy: Evidence from Colombia. *The Journal of Economic Asymmetries*, *31*, e00405. https://doi.org/10.10 16/j.jeca.2025.e00405

Ayadi, M. A., Walid Ben Omrane, & Khan, R. (2025). Intraday impact of macroeconomic and COVID-19 news on Latin American stock indexes. *Global Finance Journal*, *65*, 101103. https://d oi.org/10.1016/j.gfj.2025.101103

Baker, H. K., Hatem Rjiba, Saadi, S., & Sassi, S. (2024). Does litigation risk matter for the choice between bank debt and public debt? *Journal of Corporate Finance*, *89*, 102688. https://doi.org/ 10.1016/j.jcorpfin.2024.102688

Bansak, C., Glebocki, H., & Simpson, N. B. (2025). The impact of the U.S. Covid-19 response on remittance flows to emerging markets and developing economies. *International Economics*, *182*, 100580. https://doi.org/10.1016/j.inteco.2025.100580

Barman, S., & Jitendra Mahakud. (2024). Corporate social responsibility and financial performance: Do group affiliation and mandatory corporate social responsibility norms matter? *IIMB Management Review*, *36*, 3. https://doi.org/10.1016/j.iimb.202 4.06.003

Belkhir, M., & Sabri Boubaker. (2013). CEO inside debt and hedging decisions: Lessons from the U.S. banking industry. *Journal of International Financial Markets, Institutions and Money*, *24*, 223–246. https://doi.org/10.1016/j.intfin.2012.11.009

Bellet, C. S. (2024). The McMansion effect: Positional externalities in U.S. suburbs. *Journal of Public Economics*, *238*, 105174. https://doi.org/10.1016/j.jpubeco.2024.105174

Benedicto Kulwizira Lukanima, Sanchez-Barrios, L. J., & Yuli Paola Gómez-Bravo. (2024). Towards understanding MILA stock markets integration beyond MILA: New evidence between the pre-Global financial crisis and the COVID19 periods. *International Review of Economics & Finance*, *89*, 478–497. https://do i.org/10.1016/j.iref.2023.07.029

Blumenberg, E., Speroni, S., Siddiq, F., & Wasserman, J. L. (2024). Putting automobile debt on the map: Race and the geography of automobile debt in california. *Transportation Research Part A: Policy and Practice*, *190*, 104230. https://doi.org/10.101 6/j.tra.2024.104230

Buchanan, B. G. (2017). The way we live now: Financialization and securitization. *Research in International Business and Finance*,

39, 663–677. https://doi.org/10.1016/j.ribaf.2015.11.019

Byun, S. K., Lin, Z., & Wei, S. (2021). Are U.S. firms using more short-term debt? *Journal of Corporate Finance*, *69*, 102012. https://doi.org/10.1016/j.jcorpfin.2021.102012

Cao, P. T.-H., & Vo, D. H. (2025). Market responses to geopolitical risk and economic policy uncertainty: Evidence from Vietnam. *Heliyon*, *11*, 4. https://doi.org/10.1016/j.heliyon.2025.e42703

Cao, Q., Minetti, R., & Rowe, N. (2025). Macro-banking stability, sovereign debt and the inflation channel. *Finance Research Letters*, *78*, 107144. https://doi.org/10.1016/j.frl.2025.107144

Carrera, J., & Pablo. (2021). The impact of income inequality on public debt. *The Journal of Economic Asymmetries*, *24*, e00216. https://doi.org/10.1016/j.jeca.2021.e00216

Casteliani, L., Maki, N., & Tanaka, M. (2024). Why were disasters portrayed in postcards?: Disaster media in the early 20th century. *International Journal of Disaster Risk Reduction*, *108*, 104482. https://doi.org/10.1016/j.ijdrr.2024.104482

Chan, K. F., & Smales, L. A. (2025). U.S. Presidential news coverage: Risk, uncertainty and stocks. *International Review of Economics & Finance*, *98*, 103927. https://doi.org/10.1016/j.iref.2025.103927

Chen, L.-Y., Chen, J.-C., & Li, C.-M. (2025). Earnings informativeness, debt financing, and managerial characteristics. *International Review of Economics & Finance*, *98*, 103847. https://doi.org/10.1016/j.iref.2025.103847

Cheng, F., Gao, H., Pan, X., Qian, M., & Zhou, Q. C. (2025). China's debt market: Evolution, regulation, and global integration. *Pacific-Basin Finance Journal*, 102751. https://doi.org/10.1016/j.pacfin.2025.102751

Choi, H. M., & Swasti Gupta-Mukherjee. (2024). Public sector unions and municipal debt. *Global Finance Journal*, *60*, 100968. https://doi.org/10.1016/j.gfj.2024.100968

Claessens, S., Kose, M. A., & Terrones, M. E. (2010). The global financial crisis: How similar? How different? How costly? *Journal of Asian Economics*, *21*, 3. https://doi.org/10.1016/j.asieco.2010.02.002

Clémentine Van Effenterre. (2020). Papa does preach: Daughters and polarization of attitudes toward abortion. *Journal of Economic Behavior & Organization*, *179*, 188–201. https://doi.org/10.1016/j.jebo.2020.08.049

Clifton, T., Brewer, M., & Upenieks, L. (2023). Religious affiliation and debt among U.S. households. *Social Science Research*, *115*, 102911. https://doi.org/10.1016/j.ssresearch.2023.102911

Concepción González García. (2025). Fiscal consolidation in heavily indebted economies. *Journal of Economic Dynamics and Control*, *173*, 105046. https://doi.org/10.1016/j.jedc.2025.105046

Conny Olovsson. (2010). Quantifying the risk-sharing welfare gains of social security. *Journal of Monetary Economics*, *57*, 3. https://doi.org/10.1016/j.jmoneco.2010.02.009

Cordoba, J.-C. (2008). U.S. inequality: Debt constraints or incomplete asset markets? *Journal of Monetary Economics*, *55*, 2. https://doi.org/10.1016/j.jmoneco.2007.11.007

Corneliu Iațu, Fedor, A.-D., & Grecu, S.-P. (2024). Predictors of mayoral reelection in Romanian local elections. Long-term analysis 1996–2016. *Heliyon*, *10*, 21. https://doi.org/10.1016/j.heliyon.2024.e39812

Cumali Marangoz, Bekir Gerekan, Erdal Yılmaz, & Emre Bulut. (2025). Disentangling geopolitical risks: A quantile approach to geopolitical risk indices' impacts on stock markets. *Finance Research Letters*, *77*, 107113. https://doi.org/10.1016/j.frl.2025.10

7113

Daryna Grechyna. (2021). Mandatory spending, political polarization, and macroeconomic volatility. *European Journal of Political Economy*, *68*, 101990. https://doi.org/10.1016/j.ejpoleco.20
20.101990

Datta, S., Doan, T., & Iskandar-Datta, M. (2019). Policy uncertainty and the maturity structure of corporate debt. *Journal of Financial Stability*, *44*, 100694. https://doi.org/10.1016/j.jfs.20
19.100694

Dentler, A., & Rossi, E. (2024). Public debt management announcements: A welfare-theoretic analysis. *Economic Modelling*, *131*, 106561. https://doi.org/10.1016/j.econmod.2023.106561

Duca, J. V., & Saving, J. L. (2018). What drives economic policy uncertainty in the long and short runs: European and U. S. evidence over several decades. *Journal of Macroeconomics*, *55*, 128–145. https://doi.org/10.1016/j.jmacro.2017.09.002

Emrah Ismail Cevik, Hande Caliskan Terzioglu, Kilic, Y., Mehmet Fatih Bugan, & Sel Dibooglu. (2024). Interconnectedness and systemic risk: Evidence from global stock markets. *Research in International Business and Finance*, *69*, 102282. https://doi.org/10.1016/j.ribaf.2024.102282

Epstein, B., Nunn, R., Musa Orak, & Patel, E. (2023). Taxation, social welfare, and labor market frictions. *European Economic Review*, *151*, 104352. https://doi.org/10.1016/j.euroecorev.2022.1
04352

Ericsson, N. R. (2017). How biased are U.S. government forecasts of the federal debt? *International Journal of Forecasting*, *33*, 2. https://doi.org/10.1016/j.ijforecast.2016.09.001

Francis, B. B., Hasan, I., Jiang, C., Sharma, Z., & Zhu, Y. (2025). Climate risks and debt structure. *The British Accounting Review*, 101614. https://doi.org/10.1016/j.bar.2025.101614

French, J. J., Constantin Gurdgiev, & Shin, S. (2024). The profits vs protests: Corporate value dynamics amidst activist uproar. *Finance Research Letters*, *69*, 106263. https://doi.org/10.1016/j.frl.2024.106263

Froemel, M., & Wojtek Paczos. (2024). Imperfect financial markets and the cyclicality of social spending. *European Economic Review*, *167*, 104786. https://doi.org/10.1016/j.euroecorev.2024.104786

Fu, S., Li, E., Liao, L., Wang, Z., & Xiang, H. (2025). Unveiling the villain: Credit supply and the debt trap. *Journal of Empirical Finance*, *81*, 101592. https://doi.org/10.1016/j.jempfin.2025.101592

Gad, M., Nikolaev, V., Tahoun, A., & Lent, L. van. (2024). Firm-level political risk and credit markets. *Journal of Accounting and Economics*, *77*, 2. https://doi.org/10.1016/j.jacceco.2023.101642

Gao, L., Shi, Y., & Zheng, Y. (2025). Cryptocurrency exposure and the cost of debt. *Finance Research Letters*, *73*, 106668. https://doi.org/10.1016/j.frl.2024.106668

Garg, S., & Sushil. (2022). Impact of de-globalization on development: Comparative analysis of an emerging market (India) and a developed country (USA). *Journal of Policy Modeling*, *44*, 6. https://doi.org/10.1016/j.jpolmod.2022.10.004

Geng, X., & Qian, M. (2024). Understanding the local government debt in China. *Pacific-Basin Finance Journal*, *86*, 102456. https://doi.org/10.1016/j.pacfin.2024.102456

Gilbert, C., & Henri Guénin. (2024). The COVID-19 crisis and massive public debts: What should we expect? *Critical Perspectives on Accounting*, *98*, 102417. https://doi.org/10.1016/j.cpa.2022.102417

Gillum, R. F. (2018). *Journal of the National Medical Associa-*

tion, *110*, 5. https://doi.org/10.1016/j.jnma.2017.12.008

Gordon, R. H., & Lee, Y. (2001). Do taxes affect corporate debt policy? Evidence from U.S. corporate tax return data. *Journal of Public Economics*, *82*, 2. https://doi.org/10.1016/S0047-2727(00)00151-1

Goyal, V. K., Lehn, K., & Racic, S. (2002). Growth opportunities and corporate debt policy: the case of the U.S. defense industry. *Journal of Financial Economics*, *64*, 1. https://doi.org/10.1016/S0304-405X(02)00070-3

Grebe, M., Sinem Kandemir, & Tillmann, P. (2024). Uncertainty about the war in Ukraine: Measurement and effects on the German economy. *Journal of Economic Behavior & Organization*, *217*, 493–506. https://doi.org/10.1016/j.jebo.2023.11.015

Grigoriadis, T. N., & Torgler, B. (2009). Energy polarization and popular representation: Evidence from the Russian Duma. *Energy Economics*, *31*, 2. https://doi.org/10.1016/j.eneco.2008.10.002

Grossmann, A., & Ngo, T. (2025). The stock market reaction to bond refinancing issues with and without senior debt. *Journal of Corporate Finance*, *91*, 102746. https://doi.org/10.1016/j.jcorpfin.2025.102746

Haithem Awijen, Sami Ben Jabeur, & Houssein Ballouk. (2024). Mineral policy dynamics and their impact on equity market volatility in the global south: A multi-country analysis. *Resources Policy*, *99*, 105373. https://doi.org/10.1016/j.resourpol.2024.105373

Hall, G. J., & Sargent, T. J. (2021). *Chapter 27 - Debt and taxes in eight U.S. wars and two insurrections* ☆ ☆ *We thank William Berkley for supporting our research. Hall thanks the Theodore and Jane Norman Fund for financial support.* (A. Bisin & G. Federico, Eds.; pp. 825–880). Academic Press. https://doi.org/10.1016/B

978-0-12-815874-6.00036-8

Handl, V., & Hynek, N. (2013). Introduction. *Communist and Post-Communist Studies*, *46*, 3. https://doi.org/10.1016/j.postco mstud.2013.06.010

Hong, S. (2013). Who benefits from Twitter? Social media and political competition in the U.S. House of Representatives. *Government Information Quarterly*, *30*, 4. https://doi.org/10.1016/ j.giq.2013.05.009

Hong, Y., Zhang, R., & Zhang, F. (2024). Time-varying causality impact of economic policy uncertainty on stock market returns: Global evidence from developed and emerging countries. *International Review of Financial Analysis*, *91*, 102991. https://doi.org/ 10.1016/j.irfa.2023.102991

Hsuan, T., Salloum, A., Antti Gronow, Tuomas Ylä-Anttila, & Mikko Kivelä. (2021). Polarization of climate politics results from partisan sorting: Evidence from Finnish Twittersphere. *Global Environmental Change*, *71*, 102348. https://doi.org/10.1016/j.gloe nvcha.2021.102348

Huang, G.-Y., Shen, C. H., & Wu, Z.-X. (2023). Firm-level political risk and debt choice. *Journal of Corporate Finance*, *78*, 102332. https://doi.org/10.1016/j.jcorpfin.2022.102332

Huang, X., & Wen, H. (2025). The constraining dynamics of political instability on renewable energy development: International evidence. *Renewable Energy*, *246*, 122889. https://doi.org /10.1016/j.renene.2025.122889

Huang, Z., & Li, D. D. (2024). Public debt and debt sustainability in Europe, salary regulation in the U.S., East Asia education fever, and tax revenues of oil-rich countries. *Journal of Government and Economics*, *15*, 100123. https://doi.org/10.1016/j.jge.2024. 100123

Hurst, E., & Willen, P. (2007). Social security and unsecured

debt. *Journal of Public Economics*, *91*, 7. https://doi.org/10.1016
/j.jpubeco.2006.12.009

Huynh, N., Le, Q. N., & Tran, Q. T. (2024). Firm-level political
risk and intellectual capital investment: Does managerial ability
matter? *International Review of Financial Analysis*, *91*, 103020.
https://doi.org/10.1016/j.irfa.2023.103020

Imed Chkir, Gallali, M. I., & Manara Toukabri. (2020). Political
connections and corporate debt: Evidence from two U.S. election
campaigns. *The Quarterly Review of Economics and Finance*, *75*,
229–239. https://doi.org/10.1016/j.qref.2019.05.003

Jacobs, J. (2024). The artificial intelligence shock and socio-political polarization. *Technological Forecasting and Social Change*,
199, 123006. https://doi.org/10.1016/j.techfore.2023.123006

Jakhongir Kakhkharov, Bianchi, R. J., & Md Akhtaruzzaman.
(2024). The impact of monetary and fiscal policy on FinTech firms
during the crisis. *International Review of Economics & Finance*, *96*,
103556. https://doi.org/10.1016/j.iref.2024.103556

Ji, Q., Ma, D., Zhai, P., Fan, Y., & Zhang, D. (2024). Global
climate policy uncertainty and financial markets. *Journal of International Financial Markets, Institutions and Money*, *95*, 102047.
https://doi.org/10.1016/j.intfin.2024.102047

Joel, E., Samia Nasreen, Tiwari, A. K., & Lee, C.-C. (2023).
U.S. leveraged loan and debt markets: Implications for optimal
portfolio and hedging. *International Review of Financial Analysis*,
87, 102514. https://doi.org/10.1016/j.irfa.2023.102514

Jones, C., & Rabanal, P. (2025). Credit Cycles, fiscal policy, and
global imbalances. *Journal of International Economics*, 104063.
https://doi.org/10.1016/j.jinteco.2025.104063

Jones, J. B., & Li, Y. (2023). Social Security reform with hetero-
geneous mortality. *Review of Economic Dynamics*, *48*, 320–344.
https://doi.org/10.1016/j.red.2022.06.003

Jung, H., & Choi, S. (2024). Debt maturity and the marginal value of cash holdings. *Finance Research Letters*, *70*, 106352. https://doi.org/10.1016/j.frl.2024.106352

Kalimanshi Nsakaza, & Talumba Ireen Chilipaine. (2025). Can aid foster Africa's attainment of a just energy transition and external debt sustainability? *Heliyon*, *11*, 4. https://doi.org/10.1016/j.heliyon.2025.e42507

Kim, S., Ryu, S., Kim, Y.-S., & Lee, M.-H. (2023). How housing welfare policies impact housing cost burdens: An analysis of housing welfare policy efficacy and household characteristics. *Habitat International*, *140*, 102923. https://doi.org/10.1016/j.habitatint.2023.102923

Kock, N., & Tarkom, A. (2024). A theoretical concept of cryptocurrencies employing proof of socially beneficial work. *Technological Forecasting and Social Change*, *207*, 123628. https://doi.org/10.1016/j.techfore.2024.123628

Kramer, S., & Previts, G. J. (2015). Ivar Kreuger and IMCO: A case of taxation of fictitious income. *The International Journal of Accounting*, *50*, 3. https://doi.org/10.1016/j.intacc.2015.07.004

LaPan, C., & Xu, S. (2024a). Pluralities of agritourism: Exploring political values and social judgements. *Journal of Rural Studies*, *111*, 103395. https://doi.org/10.1016/j.jrurstud.2024.103395

LaPan, C., & Xu, S. (2024b). Pluralities of agritourism: Exploring political values and social judgements. *Journal of Rural Studies*, *111*, 103395. https://doi.org/10.1016/j.jrurstud.2024.103395

Li, H., & Chen, H. (2024). Hierarchical mortality forecasting with EVT tails: An application to solvency capital requirement. *International Journal of Forecasting*, *40*, 2. https://doi.org/10.1016/j.ijforecast.2022.08.007

Li, X., Zhou, Y., Zhu, D., & Ge, X. (2024). Research on effect of extreme climates penalties local government debt pricing: Evidence from urban investment bonds in China. *The North American Journal of Economics and Finance, 73*, 102195. https://doi.org/10.1016/j.najef.2024.102195

Lippert, A. M., Houle, J. N., & Walsemann, K. M. (2022). Student debt and cardiovascular disease risk among U.S. adults in early mid-life. *American Journal of Preventive Medicine, 63*, 2. https://doi.org/10.1016/j.amepre.2022.02.002

Liu, L., Zheng Lü, & Yoon, S.-M. (2025). Impact of policy uncertainty on stock market volatility in the China's low-carbon economy. *Energy Economics, 141*, 108056. https://doi.org/10.1016/j.eneco.2024.108056

Lotter, J. T., Ierardi, A. M., & Nembhard, M. D. (2024). *Overview of occupational safety and health regulations in the United States* (P. Wexler, Ed.; Fourth Edition, pp. 203–210). Academic Press. https://doi.org/10.1016/B978-0-12-824315-2.00968-4

Marsella, A. J. (2011). The united states of america: "A culture of war." *International Journal of Intercultural Relations, 35*, 6. https://doi.org/10.1016/j.ijintrel.2011.09.007

Martín Ardanaz, Ulloa-Suárez, C., & Valencia, O. (2024). Why don't we follow the rules? Drivers of compliance with fiscal policy rules in emerging markets. *Journal of International Money and Finance, 142*, 103046. https://doi.org/10.1016/j.jimonfin.2024.103046

McDougal, T. L., & Patterson, J. H. (2021). The global financial burden of humanitarian disasters: Leveraging GDP variation in the age of climate change. *International Journal of Disaster Risk Reduction, 55*, 102073. https://doi.org/10.1016/j.ijdrr.2021.102073

McNally, R. J., & Frueh, B. C. (2013). Why are Iraq and Afghanistan War veterans seeking PTSD disability compensation at unprecedented rates? *Journal of Anxiety Disorders, 27*, 5. http s://doi.org/10.1016/j.janxdis.2013.07.002

Milosh, M., Painter, M., Konstantin Sonin, Dijcke, D. V., & Wright, A. L. (2021). Unmasking partisanship: Polarization undermines public response to collective risk. *Journal of Public Economics*, *204*, 104538. https://doi.org/10.1016/j.jpubeco.2021.1 04538

Mishra, A. K., Ansari, Y., Bansal, R., & Maurya, P. K. (2024). Regional and periodic asymmetries in the effect of Russia-Ukraine war on global stock markets. *Heliyon*, *10*, 7. https://doi.org/10.1 016/j.heliyon.2024.e28362

Niall O'Donnell, Shannon, D., & Sheehan, B. (2023). A vaccine for volatility? An empirical analysis of global stock markets and the impact of the COVID-19 vaccine. *The Journal of Economic Asymmetries*, *28*, e00331. https://doi.org/10.1016/j.jeca.2023.e00331

Nishiyama, S. (2011). The budgetary and welfare effects of tax-deferred retirement saving accounts. *Journal of Public Economics*, *95*, 11. https://doi.org/10.1016/j.jpubeco.2011.07.010

Ogasawara, K., & Igarashi, E. (2025). The impacts of the gender imbalance on the marriage market: Evidence from World War II in Japan. *Labour Economics*, *92*, 102653. https://doi.org/10.1016/j .labeco.2024.102653

Ogwu, S. O., Okolo, C. V., & Agan, B. (2025). The role of debt burden, green financing, and energy efficiency in reducing carbon footprints in MINT & BRICS economies: New evidence from panel QARDL method. *Sustainable Futures*, *9*, 100417. https:// doi.org/10.1016/j.sftr.2024.100417

Panagiotis Karavitis, & Pantelis Kazakis. (2022). Political sentiment and syndicated loan borrowing costs of multinational enterprises. *Journal of International Financial Markets, Institutions and Money*, *78*, 101537. https://doi.org/10.1016/j.intfin.2022.1 01537

Park, Y. S. (2011). The social welfare reform during the progressive regimes of South Korea: Theoretical implications. *The Social Science Journal*, *48*, 1. https://doi.org/10.1016/j.soscij.2010.04.0 03

Patra, S., & Malik, K. (2025). Return and volatility connectedness among US and Latin American markets: A QVAR approach with implications for hedging and portfolio diversification. *Global Finance Journal*, *65*, 101094. https://doi.org/10.1016/j.gfj.2025 .101094

Richter, A. W., & Throckmorton, N. A. (2015). The consequences of an unknown debt target. *European Economic Review*, *78*, 76–96. https://doi.org/10.1016/j.euroecorev.2015.05.002

Ristolainen, K., Roukka, T., & Nyberg, H. (2024). A thousand words tell more than just numbers: Financial crises and historical headlines. *Journal of Financial Stability*, *70*, 101209. https://doi .org/10.1016/j.jfs.2023.101209

Rouhani, O. M., Geddes, R. R., Do, W., Gao, H. O., & Arash Beheshtian. (2018). Revenue-risk-sharing approaches for public-private partnership provision of highway facilities. *Case Studies on Transport Policy*, *6*, 4. https://doi.org/10.1016/j.cstp.2018.04 .003

Ruwan Lasantha, Tawiah, V., Muhammad Atif, Prem Puwanenthiren, & Nadarajah, S. (2024). Unveiling the impact of foreign competition on the bond market: Insights from S&P debt ratings. *Economics Letters*, *241*, 111797. https://doi.org/10.1016 /j.econlet.2024.111797

Schwimmer, E., Gomez-Ibanez, J. A., & Casady, C. (2019). Toll-managed lane pioneers: Lessons from five US states. *Case Studies on Transport Policy*, *7*, 3. https://doi.org/10.1016/j.cstp. 2019.05.001

Segarra, I., Atanasova, C., & Figuerola-Ferretti, I. (2024). Electricity markets regulations: The financial impact of the global energy crisis. *Journal of International Financial Markets, Institutions and Money*, *93*, 102008. https://doi.org/10.1016/j.intfin.2024.1 02008

Serhan Cevik, & João Tovar Jalles. (2023). For whom the bell tolls: Climate change and income inequality. *Energy Policy*, *174*, 113475. https://doi.org/10.1016/j.enpol.2023.113475

Shah, Y., Liu, Y., Shah, F., Shah, F., Satti, M. I., Evans Asenso, Shabaz, M., & Irshad, A. (2023). COVID-19 and commodity effects monitoring using financial & machine learning models. *Scientific African*, *21*, e01856. https://doi.org/10.1016/j.sciaf.20 23.e01856

Simonetti, J. A. (2025). *Chapter 5 - firearm suicide*☆ (N. D. Thomson, Ed.; pp. 59–74). Academic Press. https://doi.org/10 .1016/B978-0-323-95272-9.00021-8

Singh, R., Goyal, A., & Sinha, S. (2025). Global insights into biochar: Production, sustainable applications, and market dynamics. *Biomass and Bioenergy*, *194*, 107663. https://doi.org/1 0.1016/j.biombioe.2025.107663

Teschner, N., Said, H., & Shapira, S. (2024). Energy poverty and ethnic disparities among Jewish and Muslim households in Israel: The implications for welfare systems. *Energy Research & Social Science*, *116*, 103689. https://doi.org/10.1016/j.erss.2024.103689

Thi, A. (2024). From global tensions to regional integration: An analysis of bond market convergence in East Asia. *Borsa Istanbul Review*, *24*, 6. https://doi.org/10.1016/j.bir.2024.06.006

Vijverberg, C.-P. C. (2024). Income inequality and household debt: A U.S. state-level spatial analysis. *Economic Modelling*, *138*, 106772. https://doi.org/10.1016/j.econmod.2024.106772

Vogt, D., Borowski, S., Maguen, S., Blosnich, J. R., Hoffmire, C. A., Bernhard, P. A., Iverson, K. M., & Schneiderman, A. (2022).

Strengths and vulnerabilities: Comparing post-9/11 U.S. veterans' and non-veterans' perceptions of health and broader well-being. *SSM - Population Health*, *19*, 101201. https://doi.org/10.1016/j.ssmph.2022.101201

Wang, L. (2024). Partisan conflict and corporate credit spreads: The role of political connection. *Journal of Corporate Finance*, *84*, 102526. https://doi.org/10.1016/j.jcorpfin.2023.102526

Wang, Z., Ma, D., & Tang, J. (2024). Asymmetric fiscal policies and digital economy development: An empirical analysis based on the global digital value chain perspective. *International Review of Financial Analysis*, *96*, 103556. https://doi.org/10.1016/j.irfa.2024.103556

Ward, K. P., Chang, O. D., & Lee, S. J. (2025). "Tell me what I'm doing wrong": Criticism of parenting choices and mental health during COVID-19. *Early Childhood Research Quarterly*, *70*, 243–253. https://doi.org/10.1016/j.ecresq.2024.10.008

Whealin, J. M., Fischer, I. C., Na, P. J., & Pietrzak, R. H. (2023). COVID-19-related media consumption and posttraumatic stress symptoms in U.S. military veterans: A nationally representative, longitudinal study. *Psychiatry Research*, *326*, 115354. https://doi.org/10.1016/j.psychres.2023.115354

Yoon, G. (2012). War and peace: Explosive U.S. public debt, 1791–2009. *Economics Letters*, *115*, 1. https://doi.org/10.1016/j.econlet.2011.11.020

Yunus, N. (2025). Effects of oil shocks on global securitized real estate markets. *Finance Research Letters*, 106871. https://doi.org/10.1016/j.frl.2025.106871

Zhang, J. K., Botterbush, K. S., Kazimir Bagdady, Lei, C. H., Mercier, P., & Mattei, T. A. (2022). Blast-related traumatic brain injuries secondary to thermobaric explosives: Implications for the war in ukraine. *World Neurosurgery*, *167*, 176-183.e4. https://d

oi.org/10.1016/j.wneu.2022.08.073

Zhang, L., & Zhao, H. (2025). From excessive spending to debt delinquency: Should we blame mobile payments? *Computers in Human Behavior*, *165*, 108533. https://doi.org/10.1016/j.chb.2024.108533

www.ingramcontent.com/pod-product-compliance
Lightning Source LLC
Chambersburg PA
CBHW030515210326

41597CB00013B/919